*Comrade Loves of
the Samurai and
Songs of the Geishas*

EASTERN LOVE

COMRADE LOVES OF THE SAMURAI

by Saikaku Ihara

and Songs of the Geishas

English versions of "Comrade Loves of the Samurai"
and of "Japanese Songs of the Geishas" by
E. POWYS MATHERS

with an introduction to the new edition by
TERENCE BARROW, Ph.D.

CHARLES E. TUTTLE COMPANY
Rutland, Vermont & Tokyo, Japan

Representatives

British Isles & Continental Europe:

SIMON & SCHUSTER INTERNATIONAL GROUP, *London*

Australasia: BOOKWISE INTERNATIONAL
1 Jeanes Street, Beverley, 5009, South Australia

Published by the Charles E. Tuttle Co., Inc.
of Rutland, Vermont & Tokyo, Japan
with editorial offices at
Suido 1-chome, 2-6, Bunkyo-ku, Tokyo, Japan

Copyright in Japan, 1972, by Charles E. Tuttle Co., Inc.

Library of Congress Catalog Card No. 70-184817

International Standard Book No. 0-8048-1024-9

First edition published 1928 by John Rodker, London
First Tuttle edition, 1972
Seventh printing, 1988

Printed in Japan

for

H. C. S.

CONTENTS

vii

Contents

INTRODUCTION TO THE NEW EDITION

THIS VOLUME WAS FIRST PUBLISHED PRIvately in London in 1928 for subscribers to a set entitled *Eastern Love*. It comprises two separate books bound together. Both books are reprinted in this edition. The first book, *Comrade Loves of the Samurai*, is a selection of stories made by the eminent translator E. Powys Mathers. It includes tales from several Saikaku works, notably *Glorious Tales of Pederasty, Tales of the Samurai Spirit, Tales of Duty of the Samurai*, and *Stories in Letters*. The second book is a charming anthology entitled *Songs of the Geisha*, likewise selected and translated into English by Mathers.

Ihara (or Ibara) Saikaku, author of the stories of *Comrade Loves of the Samurai*, ranks as Japan's greatest novelist. His tale *Life of a Satyr* (1682) is Japan's first true novel. Born in 1642 among the merchants of Osaka, Saikaku became absorbed in the commercial world around him. In the Tokugawa era, which was launched in 1603 under the Edo shogunate, society turned away from medieval ideals to trade and moneymaking. The code of *bushido* and the knightly samurai declined in importance. Family security and personal pleasure gave a new meaning to a society that savored peace after centuries of devastating clan wars. The roots of modern Japanese are in the Tokugawa era and the Meiji era, which followed in 1868.

The best recent exposition of Ihara Saikaku's place in the Japanese literary tradition may be read in A. M. Janeira's *Japanese and Western Literature* (Charles E. Tuttle). Janeira, in his chapter "The Picaresque Novel," explains how Saikaku (with Kiseki and Ikku) introduced "a new literary genre that expressed the new social changes which were taking place." The new authors were despised by the "official" writers of the day but not by the common reading public, who preferred them in daily reading, however much they continued to venerate the classic authors. The best pictorial representation of the times is the ukiyo-e, or woodblock, art of the time, for there we see the "floating world" in which Saikaku lived and died. In many respects the novels of Saikaku are entirely modern in spirit. The character sketches in his novels have social meaning for the Japanese as those of Dickens have for the English. The genius of both may be shared by the world. The translations in *The Comrade Loves of the Samurai* were rendered by E. Powys Mathers from a French translation by Ken Sato.

Saikaku admired the merchants of his times

both for their sagacity in business and for their manner of squandering profits on a gay life. His themes are various. In the novel *This Scheming World* (Charles E. Tuttle) we see the merchants of Osaka, Edo, and Kyoto in all the rush and befuddlement of meeting year-end money obligations, and no one who has lived in Japan at year's end will fail to appreciate the subtle humor of this tale. The subject of money and love predominates in most of the incomparable stories by Saikaku. However, the love he writes about is not always that which present-day society regards as "normal."

In *Comrade Loves of the Samurai* the theme is the homosexual love of samurai for samurai or the love of samurai for page or court boy bent on becoming a samurai. The subject is potentially sordid, and in modern novels is almost invariably so, but to the old Japanese such love among samurai was quite permissible. The sons of samurai families were urged to form homosexual alliances while youth lasted, and often these loves matured into lifelong companionships. Modern samurai films and television shows often use the undying companionship of two men, but the homosexual origins of traditional relationships are overlooked by most viewers.

The homosexual loves of the samurai ranged

from those of high platonic ideal to sensual pederasty. The general attitude toward women was similar to that of classic Greece, namely that women were for breeding but boys were for pleasure. Women, in both cultures, were thought to make men cowardly, effeminate, and weak. Saikaku describes Japanese love scenes of all kinds with a frankness that has made him a favorite of the expurgators, but he touches the subject of both normal and abnormal love with tenderness. He avoids gross language and pornography, but his attitude to women is unsympathetic by modern standards. For example, in a jesting preface to *Glorious Tales of Pederasty* he says: "Our eyes are soiled by the soft haunches and scarlet petticoats of women. These female beauties are good for nothing save to give pleasure to old men in lands where there is not a single good-looking boy. If a man is interested in women, he can never know the joys of pederasty."

Homosexual males have always existed in Japan, and they figure large today, as in American society. In the traditional setting they were highly regarded, as in Polynesia, where they attached themselves to groups of chiefly women who cultivated them for both gossip and humor. They are adroit at handling social situations and succeeding in certain professions. In the modern setting homosexualism among males is driven under the surface, but it re-emerges in various guises. Love of military uniforms, jackboots, Nazi symbols, body-contact sports, muscle building, and militaristic activities is often based on this suppressed impulse. This is not to suggest that the manly soldier with wife and children at home is a homosexual, although there are curious connections between a passion for militarism and homosexuality. For example, Yukio Mishima represents a strange admixture of the *bushido* spirit and the homosexual urge to love comrades in arms with intense devotion to a cause. Mishima's tragic last act of ritual suicide, in which a comrade struck off his head, is in keeping with traditional samurai practice. In fact this anachronistic act had an enormous impact on the contemporary Japanese, since it struck a responsive cord in their latent traditional behavior patterns.

The idea of homosexuality is traditionally much more acceptable to Orientals than to Westerners. One reason for this may be the lesser physical differentiation of the sexes in the Mongoloid race (Japanese women and men have relatively sparse body hair, while women's breasts and buttocks are small compared to those of average Caucasian women.) Also the

East viewed sexual love detached from Western-style notions of sin. Provided social proprieties were observed, there was no association of sin with sex. Women were excluded from important arts (including Kabuki and Noh acting and the tea ceremony) because they were of little social importance. In the circumstances it was fitting that men should seek men for their most intimate life.

Ihara Saikaku's youthful writings were unsuccessful, but when he published his novel *The Armorous Life of Yonosuke,* the gateway to fame and prosperity opened to him. Among his many popular bawdy best sellers is *Five Women Who Loved Love* (Charles E. Tuttle).

The *Songs of the Geisha* is quite unassociated with the stories of Ihara Saikaku. It is a collection of geisha folk songs composed to be sung to the accompaniment of the shamisen. Ninety of these songs were retranslated by E. Powys Mathers from Gaston Morphy's anthology *Le Livre des Geisha.* The remainder are from *Chansons des Geishas* by Steinilber Oberlin and Hidetake Iwamura. All have that charmingly nostalgic quality which fitted well the time and the circumstances for which they were composed. Geisha entered the entertainment trade in old Japan under sad circumstances, most often being sold to procurers by impoverished parents for training in the ways of pleasure houses (for the whole story see De Becker's *The Nightless City* (Charles E. Tuttle).

For lonely girls who were courtesans and geisha the only hope was to find a lover to purchase their freedom, but until this happened —which was rare—they were obliged to spend many years in erotic slavery. When youthful bloom had faded and their time of service had expired, they were often cast aside undesired. So these songs, freely composed and intimately personal, expressed the feelings of the geisha toward their sympathetic listeners. Unlike classic songs, they reach to the heart of the common people. Love, frustration, and the futility of hope are their main themes. Here is an example from "Who Loves":

> A body that loves
> Is fragile and uncertain,
> A floating boat.
> The fires in the fishing boat at night
> Burn red, my heart burns red.
> Wooden stakes hold up the nets
> Against the tide of Uji.
>
> The tide is against me.

These song-poems, mere thumbnail sketches of life, belong to a very ancient oral tradition in Japan. The best known are popularly quoted and sung, but for a true rendering they must be heard from a beautiful geisha with a shamisen, and in a teahouse. The effect is unique. After long training in singing, dancing, and playing instruments, the geisha became herself a living work of art. These lyrics, for all their erotic symbolism, are restrained and tactful. Their erotic beauty must be felt rather than heard.

Ihara (or Ibara) Saikaku, whose real name was probably Hirayama Togo, was born in Osaka, 1642. As a poet and novelist he was one of the most illustrious writers of Japan's seventeenth-century literary revival. He excelled in describing the life of the common people and, in satirical tone, the samurai, who were in his age falling from positions of grace before the money power of the merchants.

Saikaku's speed in composing was such that he earned the nickname of "the 20,000 poet" by composing a verse a minute in twenty-four hours. Regardless of his great skill as a haiku poet, he is best known as a storyteller. His style is allusive and elliptic, accurately describing the common people among whom he lived. Society of the time was enjoying peace after years of bitter clan warfare. At last people could go about their business in comparative tranquility. The merchants and their affairs in the gay quarters gave Saikaku his most fruitful theme: that of money and love.

Some of his novels about samurai allowed his satirical humor to reach its fullness. His knack of delineating character with a few strokes of his brush enabled him to demolish knightly pretense, just as Cervantes had done in Europe, using Don Quixote and Sancho Panza. Saikaku gained popularity in his lifetime, and it has continued unabated since his death in 1693. The homosexual loves of the samurai open a window to a little understood aspect of old Japan. The love of boys and comrades is no new thing to the Western world, as its own classic culture is imbued with the idea from the days of ancient Greece. Saikaku provides us with a new view of homosexual love, which has a venerable history in Japan.

Edward Powys Mathers was born in England in 1892. He graduated from Oxford with a bachelor of arts degree after an outstanding undergraduate career at Trinity College. Following his natural inclination to literature, he became a professional author, specializing in the translation of Oriental works. From 1919 to 1931 Mathers produced many books. Among his brilliant translations from the classics the best known is *The Book of the Thousand Nights and One Night,* but his other translations, such as those of Flaubert's *Salammbô* and *The Elegies of Ovid,* rank high among his literary works taken from foreign tongues. He died in 1939.

The present tales and songs are from E. Powys Mathers' masterly anthology entitled *Eastern Love,* which was published between 1927 and 1930. This monumental collection of erotic stories expresses, as no others can, the great industry of Powys Mathers and his sensitivity to that persuasive influence over all of life— the power of love!

Terence Barrow Ph.D.

Comrade-Loves
of the Samurai
by Saïkaku Ihara

Love Vowed to the Dead

THE SHYÔGUN* YOSHIMASA, A FORMER RULER
of Japan, had, beside a passionate general
love for all arts and delicate pleasures, a par-
ticular love for incense. He had made a col-
lection of the various incense from the trees of
every province of Japan, and his sense of smell
was so nice that he could appreciate the most
subtle difference in their perfume.

One cold autumn evening he was talking with
his friends of his dear incense. Night was
drawing on, and a breath of air came suddenly
into the room carrying a soft and delicious
scent. Neither he nor his friends had ever
known so tender a perfume. He ordered one
of his attendants to search the palace for its
origin ; but it could not be found in the palace.
Then he sent his favourite, Toshikiyo Tambano-
kami, to find out where that incense burned, and
he immediately set out with his two servants.

The scent was very faint, but, when they had
crossed the meadows to the bank of the river
Kamo, it became stronger. It floated from the
other bank of the river, so Toshikiyo crossed by
a ford. This was the evening of the sixth of
November, and dark, for there was no moon.
They crossed the river by the pale light of the

stars set high in heaven. On the other bank they found a man seated upon a rock, wearing an old cloak made of straw and a rush hat. In his sleeves he held a censer. He had an air of peace and serenity.

Toshikiyo asked him : ' Dear stranger, why are you alone in such a place so late at night ? ' And while he was speaking, he smelt the perfume for which he sought, rising from the stranger's censer.

The other replied : ' I am watching the flight of the river Kamo's singing plovers.'

Toshikiyo was impressed by this answer. . To be able to listen to the plovers of the river on so cold and dark a night, the man must be finely cultured and could not be of low class. He said to him more politely : ' Excuse my curiosity, but I come at the command of my master, the Shyôgun Yoshimasa, to seek the man who diffuses so sweet a perfume. Who are you, stranger ? '

The man answered : ' I am not a priest who has renounced all worldly matters for the love of Buddha. Neither am I an ordinary man. Behold me rather a traveller, with no place to lay my head. I am more than sixty-six years old, but my feet are still firm and I can walk freely.' And he arose and started toward the pines by the water side.

It was a plain reply, yet full of mystery. Toshi-kiyo was even more surprised than before; he held the stranger back and asked him: ' I beg you to tell me the name of the incense you burn. My master Yoshimasa would like to know it.'

The man answered: ' Are you then so eager to know a trifle ? If your master is thus fond of incense, take him this, although there is not much more of it.' And, giving him the incense and the censer, he went quickly away.

Toshikiyo came back with the incense and censer to Yoshimasa and told his master every detail of the strange old man. The Shyôgun was greatly intrigued by the stranger's refine-ment and had him sought through the whole of Kyoto ; but no trace of the old man was found. The Shyôgun was grieved at this, and kept his gift with the utmost care. He named that incense ' The Plover,' and the strange story soon spread among his attendants.

One of Yoshimasa's pages, the son of a samurai of an Eastern Province, had so beautiful a face that even the flowers of Kyoto grew pale before him. He was one of the Shyôgun's favourite lads. When he saw the censer his countenance changed suddenly, and he was seized with great distress. His name was Gorokitji Sakurai. His closest friend asked him why the sight of the censer had so moved him, but Gorokitji would not open his heart. Now this friend was his very dear lover.

His distress finally made Gorokitji ill, and, on his bed, he confided at last in his friend, whose name was Muranosuke Higutji. Gorokitji's voice was weak and shook as he told of his past life and how it was concerned with the censer:

' The owner of this incense was my lover. We loved each other with unchangeable love. But he thought that our love might be harmful to my career, and therefore he left me in that Eastern land and came to Kyoto. But I could not forget him. I followed him here as a page of our master Yoshimasa, hoping and waiting for a blessing of Providence to let me meet him once again. But fortune was not with me. I have met only the censer; I have not met him to whom it belonged, him whom I love.' And Gorokitji wept many bitter tears.

Muranosuke was very sorrowful. He was afraid of losing his friend and lover if Gorokitji should die. And yet Gorokitji grew weaker and weaker, until there was no more hope of his living. Then he called Muranosuke to his bedside and said : ' Dear Muranosuke, find that old man after my death and love him in my place. Because you have been my best friend I ask you this unpleasing and indelicate favour.

I beg you to perform my last wish, for the love of my soul which is about to leave you. If you refuse it this favour, it will not be able to ascend into Heaven.'

This prayer was truly unreasonable, but Gorokitji and Muranosuke were friends and lovers, and were bound to sacrifice their lives for each other. Therefore Muranosuke promised, and Gorokitji could die with a smile. He was mourned and regretted by all his friends, some of whom could not restrain their sobs on seeing his beautiful, lifeless face. His body was burned on the hill Toribe, and only his bones remained as witness to his earthly existence.

After a long and arduous search, Muranosuke at last found the old man, living in a hut with a broken roof and two doors which would hardly shut. It was girt by a low evergreen hedge. On a rainy evening Muranosuke visited him.

It had been a dreary, desolate day, and the man had been thinking of Gorokitji; for his love of the youth was so deep that he could not forget him. Muranosuke told him of his friend's death, and the old man was seized with a great despair. He kept on sobbing: 'I would that this news were many times false.' When he was a little calmer, Muranosuke looked at him to tell him of the promise he had given to his dying friend. The old man's face was

7

decomposed and wasted. He was more than sixty years old. To love such a man was very repulsive to Muranosuke. But he had sworn at Gorokitji's death-bed to love the creature in his friend's place, and he was bound by the honour of a samurai to fulfill his promise. So he said to the old man :

' Dear stranger, when our friend Gorokitji was dying, he prayed me to seek you out and love you in his stead. Love me, then, in place of my friend Gorokitji. Let us be lovers.'

The old man was greatly surprised by this sudden proposal. He raised his tear-bathed face and answered :

' Your proposition is quite unexpected. I adore my poor Gorokitji, and cannot accept your love. Also I am too old to be your lover. I am touched by your attachment to Gorokitji ; but excuse me from accepting this offer.'

For a long time he refused, until Muranosuke said to him despairingly : ' I must fulfill my promise to my dead friend. If you refuse to perform his last wish, I have only one way to save my honour as a samurai. I must perform Harakiri, for I am not so base as to outlive the breach of a promise.'

Then the old man regretfully agreed to accept Muranosuke's love. He was touched by such loyalty, and could not refuse to accomplish the last wish of their beloved Gorokitji. So they vowed a lifelong love and friendship to each other, and Muranosuke visited the old man every evening.

When this story became known, everyone praised Muranosuke's conduct and his loyal passion for the old man. He did not love him, but he kept him as his lover solely to fulfill his promise to Gorokitji.

2

All Comrade-Lovers die by Hara-kiri

THE FAIREST PLANTS AND TREES MEET THEIR death because of the marvel of their flowers. And it is the same with humanity : many men perish because they are too beautiful.

There was a page named Ukyo-Itami, who served a Lord at Yedo. He was cultured and elegant, and so extremely beautiful that he troubled the eyes of those who looked at him. His master had another page named Uneme Mokawa, eighteen years of age, who also had great beauty and a countenance full of graces. Ukyo was so smitten with this other as almost to lose his senses, so moved was he by his virile loveliness. He suffered to such an extent from his love that he fell ill and had to take to his bed, where he sighed and moaned his unheard love in solitude. But he was very popular, and many people had pity on him and came to see him in his illness, to care for him and console him.

One day his fellow-pages came to visit him, and among them was his beloved Uneme. At sight of him, Ukyo betrayed by his expression the sentiments which he felt for him, and the pages then guessed the secret of his illness. Samanosuke Shiga, another page who was Uneme's lover, was also present, and was much moved at seeing the suffering of poor Ukyo. He stayed with the invalid when the others went away, knelt down beside him and whispered : ' I am sure, dear Ukyo, that there is a grief in your soul. Open your heart to me who am your friend and love you very much. Do not keep any secret from me : you only torture yourself by keeping it. If you love any of the pages who were here just now, tell me frankly. I shall do my best to help you, Ukyo.'

But the bashful Ukyo could not open his sick heart to him. He simply said : ' You are wrong, my Samanosuke, you are mistaken about me,' and, since Samanosuke insisted, he pretended to be asleep. Samanosuke went away.

They caused two High Priests to pray for Ukyo's recovery, and after they had prayed without ceasing for two days and two nights Ukyo seemed better. Then Samanosuke again went secretly to Ukyo and said : ' Dear friend, write him a love-letter. I will give it to him without fail, and he shall at once send you a kind answer. I know whom you love so desperately, and you need not consider me in your passion. He and I are lovers, but I am quite ready to satisfy your desire, because of our long and sincere friendship, Ukyo.'

Then Ukyo took courage and wrote a letter with trembling hand, and entrusted it to Samanosuke. When Samanosuke reached the palace he met Uneme, who was looking in silence at the flowers in the garden. Uneme saw him, and said : 'Dear friend, I have been very busy every evening amusing my Lord with Nô plays, and this evening I have only come out for a few moments to breathe a little air. I have read my master the ancient classical poem " Seuin Kokin," and was alone and without a friend except for the silent cherry blooms. I am very lonely.' And he looked tenderly at Samanosuke.

' Here is another silent flower, Uneme,' said Samanosuke, and held out the letter to him.

Uneme smiled at him and said : ' This letter cannot be for me, dear friend.' He went behind some thick trees to read it. He was touched by the letter, and kindly replied to Samanosuke : ' I cannot remain unmoved if he suffers so much for me.'

When Ukyo received Uneme's answer, he was filled with joy, and quickly recovered his health. And the three young men loved each other with a loyal and harmonious love.

Now it happened that their master took into his service a new courtier named Shyuzen Hosono. This man was rough, evil, and of a hasty temper; he had no finesse or elegance; he was continually boasting of his exploits, and no one liked him. When he saw Ukyo he fell in love with him; but he had not the delicacy to make his love known to him in some charming letter: he had not sufficiently good taste for that. He pursued Ukyo with smiles and tears whenever he saw him alone in the palace or the garden. But Ukyo despised him.

The Lord had a servant with his head shaven, whose duty it was to take care of the utensils belonging to the tea ritual. He was named Shyusaï Tushiki, and had become the intimate friend of Shyuzen; so he undertook to convey a message from him to Ukyo. Accordingly he said one day to Ukyo: 'I pray you to give Shyuzen a kind answer. He loves you passionately,' and gave him Shyuzen's letter.

But Ukyo threw the letter away and said: 'It is not your business to carry love-letters. Attend to your duty of keeping the master's house clean for tea matters,' and went away.

Shyuzen and Shyusaï were consumed with rage. They determined to kill Ukyo that same night, and then to run away. They could not endure the insult and humiliation which Ukyo had inflicted upon them, and made ready for their vicious deed. But Ukyo was warned of their plot and decided to kill them both before they

could attack him. He thought of speaking to
Uneme about it, but, on reflection, told himself
that it was unworthy of a samurai to speak
about his business to his lover with the sole
object of obtaining his help. Besides, he did not
want to make Uneme his accomplice. So he
decided to execute his plan by himself.

It was the month of May and very wet. It
rained heavily on that night. It was the seven-
teenth day of the moon in the seventeenth year
of Kanyei (A.D. 1641). All the samurai of the
guard were in a state of deep fatigue, and were
sleeping. Ukyo put on a thin silk garment as
white as snow, with a splendid skirt. He per-
fumed himself more than ordinarily so as to be
pure, for he had determined to die after having
killed his two enemies. He put two swords in
the girdle which encircled his hips, and crossed
through the halls of the palace. Since he was
in the habit of doing this every evening, the
guards let him pass without questioning.

Shyuzen was on guard that night in one of the
rooms. He was leaning against a screen pic-
tured with hawks, and was looking at his fan.
Ukyo rushed upon him and thrust his sword
deep into his right shoulder as far as his breast.
But Shyuzen was a brave and strong man.
With his left hand he seized his own sword and
defended himself bravely. Yet he was losing

14

blood and getting weak, and finally he fell, cursing Ukyo. Ukyo finished him with two more sword thrusts; then he went in search of Shyusaï.

But the guards had been aroused by the noise of the struggle, and had lit lamps in the rooms. They arrested Ukyo, and their captain led him before the Lord, who was much disturbed and very angry. He spoke harshly to Ukyo and said to him: 'What reason had you for killing Shyuzen? You deserve severe punishment for having thus troubled my palace in the night with your crime. Confess your reason for having killed him.' But Ukyo kept silent. He was brought before the Chief Judge, Tonomo Tokumatsu, who examined him; and Ukyo confessed. When the Lord was informed of this, he grew calm and ordered Ukyo to be kept in a room in the palace, where he was treated with respect.

Shyuzen's father was one of the Lord's hereditary courtiers. He was so outraged by the crime committed against his son that he swore to die by Hara-kiri on the same spot where his son had fallen. His mother also was a favourite of the Princess, the Lord's wife. She used to take part in the Princess's poetical gatherings. All night, with bare feet, she wept and mourned her son's death. She besought the Princess to

punish the murderer, saying : ‘If the Lord
pardons the murderer, there is no law or justice
in the world.’

Accordingly the Lord grudgingly resolved to
condemn Ukyo to die by Hara-kiri. Shyusaï,
who had carried the message to Shyuzen, con-
trived his own death also.

Uneme had at that time received leave of
absence from his master to visit his mother at
Kanagawa, and did not know that Ukyo had
been condemned to death. But Samanosuke
wrote to him to say that Ukyo was to kill him-
self next morning at the Keiyoji temple at
Asakusa. Uneme sent Samanosuke his thanks,
and hastened at daybreak to the temple without
even taking time to bid his mother farewell.
As he stood in the chief entrance to the temple,
which was in the form of a low tower, several
people started talking noisily about Hara-kiri.
They said : ‘Early this morning a young
samurai is coming here to kill himself. They
say that he is very beautiful. Even an ugly son
is dear to his parents ; the father and mother
of this young samurai will be smitten with
despair at realising that so accomplished a son
must die. Surely it is a pity to kill such a
splendid young man.’ Uneme could hardly
restrain his tears on hearing these people. The
temple quickly filled, and he hid himself behind

a door and waited for the arrival of his darling Ukyo.

Shortly after, a fine new litter was seen to approach, borne by several men, surrounded by guards. It stopped opposite the door, and Ukyo descended from it with the utmost calmness. He was wearing a white silk garment embroidered with autumn flowers, having pale blue facings* and a skirt. He stopped for a moment and looked about him. On the tombs were some thousands of wooden tablets bearing the names of those who were buried there. Among them rose a wild cherry tree with white blossom on the upper branches only. Ukyo looked at the pale, fading flowers, and softly murmured an old Chinese poem :

> *The flowers wait for next Spring,*
> *Trusting that the same hands shall caress them.*
> *But men's hearts will no longer be the same,*
> *And you will only know that everything changes,*
> *O poor lovers.*

The seat destined for the Hara-kiri had been placed in the garden of the temple. Ukyo calmly seated himself on the gold-bordered mats and summoned his attendant, whose duty it was to cut off the condemned man's head to shorten his suffering after he had manipulated the dagger in his belly. This attendant's name was Kajuyu Kitji Kawa, and he was a courtier of the same Lord. Ukyo cut off the wonderful locks of his hair, put them in a white paper and gave them to Kajuyu, praying him to send them to his venerable mother at Horikawa in Kyoto as a keepsake. The priest then began to pray for the salvation of Ukyo's soul.

Ukyo said: 'Beauty in this world cannot endure for long. I am glad to die while I am young and beautiful, and before my countenance fades like a flower.' Then he took a green paper from his sleeve and wrote his farewell poem upon it. This was his poem:

I loved the beauty of flowers in springtime;
In autumn the glory of the moon
Was my delight;
But now that I am looking upon death face to my face,
These joys are vanishing;
They were all dreams.

Then he thrust the knife into his belly, and Kajuyu at once struck off his head from behind. At that moment Uneme ran to the mats and cried: 'Finish me also,' and pierced himself. Kajuyu struck off his head. Ukyo was sixteen years old, and Uneme eighteen. The tombs of these two young men remained for a long time in the temple, and Ukyo's farewell poem was inscribed on their joint stones. On the seven-

teenth day after their death, Samanosuke also
died by Hara-kiri, leaving a letter to say that he
could not survive his lovers' death.

Such was the tragedy of these
young men who died
for love.

3

He Followed his Friend into the Other World, after Torturing him to Death

ON THE SECOND DAY OF THE YEAR THE LORD of the Province Iga dreamed that it snowed, and on the next morning snow began to fall. He said to his attendants : ' It is snowing just as I dreamed last night.' One of the pages, named Sasanosuke Yamawaki, went into another room and brought from it a picture of Fuji Yama by the famous painter Tanyo, and hung it in the recess of the room. The Lord was delighted by this tactful and intelligent action ; for to dream that one sees the snow upon Fuji is considered by every superstitious person as a sign of happiness. He compared Sasanosuke's action with that of Seishyônajon, an ancient and famous poetess of the Imperial Court. The Emperor Tjijo had one day asked : ' What will be the appearance of Mount Koro under morning snow ? ' Then Seishyônajon quickly unrolled the bamboo blind before the north door of the palace. For a great Chinese poet says in one of his poems :

> You may hear the bells of temple Taiji
> By raising your head from the pillow,
> But to see the snows of Mount Koro
> You must unroll the blind before the door.

Sasanosuke had considerable tact and intelligence, and he gave his master great pleasure by imitating this famous lady. From that time he became one of the Lord's favourites. When the Lord departed for Yedo to pay his respects to the Shyôgun, Sasanosuke stayed in the Province and was free to do as he pleased. One day he went with three other pages to hunt birds in the fields. They walked for a long time without finding even a sparrow for their trouble, and decided to return home. But behind a clump of bamboos there was a hut where the country folk used to shelter their melons from birds and thieves during the summer, and, as the young men passed this, a pheasant flew out from it. With the help of their bamboos the pages caught the bird; and then several more pheasants flew from the hut. The young men were delighted with such a stroke of luck. But one of them was surprised to see so many pheasants, and made his way into the hut. There he saw two men hiding with a big cage full of these birds. He rebuked the men severely. 'You are committing a crime against the Lord's law. Do you not know that it is forbidden by edict for a man of the people to catch birds?'

While he was questioning the men, one of them escaped, hiding his face with his big rush straw hat. But the other was seized by the pages and stood in some danger, for the youths were very angry. But Sasanosuke interceded for the wretched man, saying : 'Perhaps these poor fellows caught the birds for food. Let us have mercy, and pardon him at least this time.'

They released the man and returned to their houses, rejoicing at this easy capture. And they tied the birds to plum tree branches. But Sasanosuke, pretending that his foot hurt him, stayed behind and, when the others were out of sight, insistently questioned the man : 'I shall not let you go until you tell me why you and your accomplice hid yourselves in this place. Be frank, and confess that something strange underlies the matter.'

The terrified man at once confessed : 'I am the slave of Hayemon Banno. My master escaped before you seized me.'

'I know Hayemon. He is, in fact, known everywhere. Why did he run away ? It is very strange.'

The slave answered : 'My master said to me this morning : " To-day Sasanosuke Yamawaki will come this way to hunt birds ; but, after all the samurai who have birded here lately, he will find them very scarce and be disappointed. I am going to provide his sport with some of my own birds." That is why my master and I loosed these birds for your pleasure.'

'This young man is very fortunate,' said Sasanosuke, 'to be so appreciated by such a man as Hayemon. I should like to be that youth.' And, taking off his robe, he gave it to the slave for a present. But the slave would have preferred the garment to have been a great bottle full of wine.

Afterwards, this fellow became the messenger between Hayemon and Sasanosuke, and enabled them to enjoy their loves, for they were both brave and honourable men.

But one autumn the tree in the garden of the temple Saïmenji on Mount Nayata bloomed for the second time. The samurai assembled at the temple to enjoy this spectacle, and made a noble pleasure party, feasting on delicious foods and wines. This caused them to forget both the flowers and themselves, and they remained till evening. There were among them several of the Lord's pages. Hayemon had also come to see the flowers and to enjoy himself with the other samurai. Itjisaburo Igarashi, one of the pages, gave him a cup of wine to drink, the half of which he had already drained himself. Hayemon thanked him with most flattering compliments, saying : 'You are a truly pretty boy. I delight in your beauty even while I am drinking.' And he let Itjisaburo fill the cup again with heady wine. When he was drunk he took his pleasure with Itjisaburo ; but, on going away, he did not forget his two swords. These are the soul of a samurai.

Someone told Sasanosuke of Hayemon's conduct with Itjisaburo, and he was shaken by anger and jealousy. The next day the weather changed suddenly, it grew cold, and a furious gale began to blow. Sasanosuke waited for Hayemon at the door of his house and, when he arrived, impatiently took him by the hand and led him to a little inner court. Then he locked the door and also every way out of the house, and left Hayemon in that yard. Hayemon thought that Sasanosuke was making ready a love meeting, and waited for some time in the court. But the snow, which had begun to fall in the early evening, was getting thicker. At first Hayemon shook the snow from his shoulders and sleeves ; but soon, although he had sheltered under an old paulownia, he began to suffer greatly. In a husky voice he called to his lover : ' Sasanosuke, I shall die of this cold.' But Sasanosuke mockingly answered him from the first-floor room, where he was amusing himself with the servant : ' I am sure that you are still sufficiently warmed by the wine that pretty page poured out for you.'

Hayemon groaned : 'You are teaching me a lesson this evening. I shall be very discreet in future. I will not look at a single other pretty boy. Forgive me, Sasanosuke.'

But Sasanosuke was unyielding. 'If you are in earnest, pass me your two swords to prove it. Only so shall I believe you.' And Hayemon passed him his two swords.

Then, to avenge his slighted love, Sasanosuke set about making game of Hayemon. He compelled him take off all his clothes. Then he forced the unhappy man, who stood shivering and naked in the cold, to let his hair fall over his face ; and Hayemon obeyed him. Sasanosuke threw him a triangular white paper with characters written on it, and ordered him to place it on his forehead. In burials, according to the Buddhistic rite, the corpse bears a triangular paper with an inscription on its forehead. And Hayemon obeyed.

The air was frozen and the snow fell upon his naked, shuddering, trembling body. He could hardly breathe. He looked like a corpse indeed. He implored Sasanosuke to forgive and save him, raising his frozen and shivering hands to him. But Sasanosuke remained pitiless. Up in his room he sang at the top of a clear and care-free voice, to the rhythm of a drum, this passage from the famous Nô drama : 'I am delighted with your excellent prayer for the safety of my soul.' Then, after this moment's inattention, he looked back into the court.

Hayemon had fallen down in pain and agony. Sasanosuke was moved and ran to the court, and tried to revive his lover with medicines and warmth. But it was too late; Hayemon had died. Sasanosuke joined him in death by Hara-kiri.

In his bedroom Sasanosuke had prepared a feast for himself and his dear Hayemon. There were the most delicious meats, and two cushions were on the bed for Hayemon and himself. His garments were perfumed. He had intended to pardon Hayemon after punishing him severely; but he had gone too far, and had thereby killed his lover and himself.

4

He Died to Save his Lover

THE SEA SUDDENLY BEGAN TO RAGE, AND the waves hurled themselves angrily upon the coast. The sky was covered with big black clouds, and the storm rushed down from Mount Muko. A violent rain began to fall, and people walking were seized with panic. Among these was a certain samurai, the ambassador of the Lord of Akashi to another Lord of a neighbouring Province. He took shelter with his servant under a big tree, and a boy, about thirteen years old, passed by them carrying a paper umbrella. Seeing the samurai under the tree, the lad gave his umbrella to the servant.

The samurai, whose name was Sakon Horikoshi, said : ' Thank you, dear child, for your kindness ; but tell me, do you not need the umbrella yourself ? ' The boy's only answer was to start weeping. Sakon asked him the reason of his grief, and, drying his tears, the other replied : ' I am the son of Sluyuzen Magasaka, and my name is Korin. My father left his Lord of the Province of Kaï, and we came to the Province of Buzen ; but he died suddenly on the boat, and my mother and I buried him in this village. Since then we have lived here in a little house which we built with the help of the obliging villagers, and we make umbrellas for a living. But I cannot use this poor umbrella to protect myself from the rain without sorrowfully thinking that my mother made it with her unfortunate, delicate hands.'

Sakon was greatly touched by this sad story, and went to the village and learned from the mother that the boy's tale was true. When he gave his message to the Governor of the Province, he spoke to him also of Korin. The Lord was moved and commanded Sakon to bring the lad before him ; so Sakon very joyfully presented the boy and his mother to that Lord. Korin was very beautiful : his young, untroubled face was like a serene moon in the autumn sky : his black hair was a lotus, and his voice had the love-murmuring of the nightingale amid young peach blossom.

The Lord made Korin his page and loved him greatly. Time passed and, one evening when Korin was on guard, the Lord tenderly caressed him and whispered : ' Dear sweet Korin, I would even give you my life if you desired it.'

But Korin answered : ' Your flatteries give me little pleasure, my Lord, since it is no true love for a samurai to have an affair with a Lord who is all-powerful. It is even a dishonour for one who esteems a selfless and sincere male love. I would rather have a man of some class for my

28

lover, it is true, but he would have to be devoted and utterly true ; a man whom I could love all my life. That would be my greatest pleasure.'

The Lord said to him : ' Come, you are not serious ! ' But Korin insisted : ' My Lord, I mean what I say, and it is the vow of my heart. I swear it on my love as a samurai and before all the gods of Japan.'

The Lord was astonished at the bold frankness of this boy.

One evening the Lord arranged a feast in a summer-house, at which his numerous and beautiful pages were present. Suddenly a suffocating breath filled the garden and caused the trees to shudder. A very great monster came down from the roof, thrusting out its horrible head to look at the company. It stretched its mighty paws and began to maul the noses of the terrified onlookers, who at once surrounded their Lord and hurried back into the palace. Then a loud noise was heard in the garden, as if a mountain had fallen. After midnight a slave came and told the Lord that an immense badger had been found with its head cut off in the tea-house in the garden. The beast was still crooking its claws when it was found, although it was dead.

' Certainly,' said the Lord, ' this evening's monster, when we were in the tea-house, was that great badger.* And the loud noise was made by the beast to frighten us. I wonder who was the brave man who dared to kill this portent.' And he questioned all his courtiers, but none of them had killed the badger.

Seven days after this incident, at about two o'clock in the morning, a maiden was heard crying on the roof of the great hall of the palace : ' Korin has killed my father the badger. He will soon die. He will fulfill his destiny.' The voice repeated this threat three times, and was silent. It was then known that Korin was the hero who had killed the badger. Everyone praised his courage, his modesty, and his heroic deed.

One of the courtiers, who had charge of the maintenance of the palace, begged the Lord to have the roof which the badger had damaged put into repair. But the Lord refused, saying : ' There was once a great Chinese Prince who was full of pride, and boasted, saying : " All my words are true, and let no one dare to act against my orders." Then one of his courtiers, called Sihkyo, who was truly loyal and devoted, struck him with a harp to rebuke him for his unconsidered words. And the Prince was grateful to him for his loyalty. He left the wall, which the harp had injured in striking him, just as it was, without any reparation. And I desire to leave the damaged roof, that all may remember and admire Korin's courage for ever.'

This adventure only served to increase the ardour of the Lord's love for Korin. Now the second son of Gyobu-Kamo, one of the Lord's courtiers, greatly admired Korin. His name was Sohatjiro ; and his admiration grew to love. He sent many amorous letters to Korin, and Korin was touched by them. But since they could not meet openly, because of the Lord, they waited for a suitable opportunity.

It was the custom to give the palace a thorough cleaning on the thirteenth of December, and for the courtiers to change their old clothes for new and spotless garments. On that day, following a plan conceived by Korin's servant, Sohatjiro was introduced into the palace in a big bamboo basket, in which Korin had already sent some new soft robes to his mother. They succeeded in carrying Sohatjiro into the room adjoining the Lord's bedroom.

Korin pretended that he had pains in the stomach, and kept the screen doors well oiled so as to be able to open them easily in the night. The first time Korin went out of the room, the Lord complained of the noise he made ; but, as the night advanced, the latter fell into a deep sleep and started to snore very loudly. Then Korin, thinking that the moment had come

31

when he might join his love, crept into the next room. The two lovers embraced and swore a faithful and changeless love until their deaths. They spoke very quietly, in a whisper, of their amorous pleasures; but by ill luck it happened that the Lord was wakened by their voices.

He shouted: 'There is someone in the next room, and he shall not escape.' He grasped a spear, which was resting against his pillow, and rushed upon Sohatjiro as he turned to run away. But Korin seized him by the sleeve and said: 'It is not worthy of you, Lord, to agitate yourself in this way. Be calm, I beg you. There was no one here but I. I was only uttering certain complaints because of my pain. Forgive me, Lord, for having disturbed your sleep.'

At that moment Sohatjiro started to climb over the wall by the help of a large branch, and the Lord saw him. He sternly questioned Korin; but the other denied everything. Then, since he had great love for Korin, the Lord thought that this was perhaps another evil badger haunting the garden, and he calmed himself.

But one of the sentinels, Shinroku Kanaï, came and said to the Lord: 'I saw the track of a man in this room, and himself with my own eyes in the garden. His hair was disordered and his actions were strange. It must be Korin's secret lover.

I advise the Lord to watch Korin.' But Korin answered bravely : ' My dear one has given me his life. He is my faithful lover. Even if I must die, I will not tell his name. I have already said this many times to my Lord.' He was calm and serene.

Two days later Korin was led into the guard-room of the palace, and the Lord said to him : ' I myself will execute you, Korin, as a warning to my courtiers not to deceive me. Prepare to die.' And he took a halberd in his hands.

Korin smiled at him : ' I thank my Lord for wishing to take my life with his own hands, in memory of our past time. I am quite ready.' And he stood up.

Then the Lord cut off his left hand, and asked : ' How do you feel, Korin ? '

Korin held out his right hand to be cut off also, and said : ' With this hand I caressed and loved my lover. You should hate this hand a great deal also.'

The Lord at once cut that hand off. Then Korin turned his back to his master and said : ' My back is very beautiful. No other page was as attractive as I am. Look at my beauty before I die.' His voice was weak and low through the mortal pain he was enduring. Then the Lord cut off his head and, holding it in his hands, wept bitter tears for the death of his favourite.

The body was buried in the cemetery of the temple Myofukuji. In this temple there was a little pool called 'Glory of the Morning.' Korin's short life was like a morning glory. Everybody accused and blamed his cowardly lover, who had remained hidden after his friend's death. They despised him as we despise a stray dog.

But next year, on the fifteenth of January, Sohatjiro killed Shinroku, who had betrayed Korin to the Lord. He cut off his two hands, as the Lord had done to Korin, and finished him by piercing his throat with his sword. He sent Korin's mother into a safe place. Then he went to the cemetery, wrote a memoir in which he recounted his love for Korin and his vengeance against Shinroku, and killed himself by Hara-kiri on his lover's tomb. As he opened his belly, he traced with his knife the armorial bearings of his Korin there. For seven days after his death his friends and admirers loaded his tomb with flowers. Korin and Sohatjiro became an illustrious example of the love of comrades.

5

The Soul of a Young Man smitten with Love follows his Lover on a Journey

IN A SPRING MEADOW STUDDED WITH GRACE-ful flowers and fresh grasses were two richly and elegantly clothed persons gathering spring flowers. Their faces were shaded by large hats.

A young man stood watching these two graceful silhouettes. He could not see their faces, and was curious to know what beautiful boys they might be. He had great longing to see their delightful faces. Then an old servant woman came out of the tent, and called to them : ' Dear maidens, dear Ofuji and Oyoshi.' The young man was disappointed to find that the two graceful persons were women and not young men. He went swiftly to the town of Sendai, the capital of that Province.

At the end of one of the streets of this town, called Bashyoja Fsuojji, there was a druggist's shop, the owner of which was a certain Hiusuke Ronishi. As our young man passed the shop, a delicious scent of incense escaped from the black curtains at the back of it, separating the commercial part from the living-rooms. The perfume was sweeter than that famous White

Chrysanthemum incense which only the Lord of the Province possessed. The young man had a keen taste in incense, and was attracted by the perfume.

So he entered the shop and, after buying some common perfumes, said to the proprietor : ' I should like to buy that incense which you are now burning behind the shop. Its perfume is exquisite. Will you give me a little ? ' But the proprietor answered : ' That incense is my son's favourite, and we cannot sell it.'

The young man was cast down, and lingered for a moment in the shop ; for he could not tear himself from the delicious odour ; and it was with regret that he withdrew. His name was Itjikuro Ban, and he was a Guard of the Province of Tsugaru, and immensely rich. He was passionately addicted to pederasty and did not waste a thought on women. He was at that particular time going to Yedo to see a celebrated young actor named Dekijima, whose beauty was attracting many men's admiration. His servant had received a letter from a friend at Yedo, praising Dekijima's beauty, and Itjikuro had at once set out to see him. He was a person of great refinement and dignity, of a rank which is seldom met with in so distant a country.

Jutaro, the druggist's son, had seen Itjikuro and fallen in love with him. He thought :

36

' My fair youth cannot last for ever, and I shall soon be a grown man. Many men love and admire me for my beauty, and I have received more than a hundred love letters ; but I have not read a single one of them. People say that I have no heart. But none of these men had any allure for me. Only this elegant male has troubled me. If he could but return my love, I should love him all my life long. In truth I love him desperately. His manly beauty has made me lose my head. He has fascinated me.' His too ardent and youthful blood so inflamed him that his passion threw him to the ground. His eyes became set, and he seemed like a madman. He rushed about, holding his long-cherished spaniel in his right hand, while he brandished a sword with the other. No one could go near him. At last, at the risk of her own life, his nurse managed to seize him. She consoled and cheered him : ' My dear young master, calm yourself ! We can recall this traveller and arrange your love. I beg you to take command of yourself, dear master.' The young man then became a little calmer. His parents engaged a travelling priest to pray for his recovery.

Hiusuke, the young man's father, had, when thirty-five years of age, married a rich merchant's daughter ; but he had reached the age of sixty without having a child. Then he and his wife prayed Tenjin to grant them a child, and remained in prayer for seven days before the shrine of the god. On the evening of the seventh day they dreamed that a blossom fell from a plum tree into the wife's mouth, and that she became with child. They were very happy and grateful to the god Tenjin. Then Jutaro was born.

He was hardly five years old when he began to write Chinese letters without ever having learned them. At thirteen he wrote a story about a meeting between two young lovers who had to separate after a short time on a summer evening. He called the book: *The Love of a Short Summer Evening*. Such was his genius.

Therefore his sudden illness caused great sorrow to his parents and friends. The priest's prayer had no great effect. Jutaro was in a continuous delirium, and grew weaker every day. His pulse became so faint that all hope of saving him was lost. His parents wove a fair white shroud and made ready a beautiful coffin for his burial; for they expected his death at any moment.

But one day, suddenly, the young man raised his weary head and said in a weak voice to his relations : ' I am happy, for this man whom I

love will pass along the street to-morrow evening. Stop him, and bring him to me.'
Those who heard him thought that he was speaking in his delirium ; but to appease him they sent a man named Biwajutji to wait for the stranger at the town gate. And lo ! as the sick man had said, the stranger arrived. They brought him to Hiusuke's house, and the father, overcome with emotion, told him of his son's strange illness.

Itjikuro was touched by this love, and said to the father : ' If your son dies, I shall become a priest, that I may pray all my life for the safety of his soul. But I wish to see him before he dies. I should like to say good-bye to him before he leaves this world.'

They entered the young man's room, and the weakened Jutaro at once sat upright on his bed, as soon as he saw him whom he loved. And he recovered immediately, and became as well as he had been before. Everybody was astonished at this thing.

Jutaro said to Itjikuro : 'My body remained here, but my soul has been with you all the time. Perhaps you have not been aware of it. Lord, I love you. One night when you had gone into the inner room at Hiraizumi, after having visited the historic places of Takadatji, my soul slept with you in the same bed and loved you without speaking a word. Then I placed a little of my special incense in your sleeve. Have you it still ? '

Itjikuro took a piece of incense from his pocket and said : ' This is indeed strange. I was glad to find this exquisite incense in my sleeve, but I could not explain whence it had come. Now I understand, and it is a miracle. I did not know that we had made a contract of love together.'

The young boy replied : ' I wish to give you a proof of that contract which will make you believe me.' He took a broken piece of incense from his pocket and, putting the two pieces together, showed that they fitted exactly ; also their perfume was the same. Itjikuro was then convinced, and they swore to love each other always, even in future existence. Itjikuro returned to his birth town, taking Jutaro on his horse, and the young boy's relations gladly agreed to give him to his lover.

.   .   .

6

The Tragic Love of Two Enemies

THE LORD OF THE PROVINCE ETJIGO WAS called Jibudayu Mashikura. One day his chief minister, Gyobu Tokuzawa, summoned his master's first page, Senpatji Akanashi, who was in the vestibule with the other pages, whispering : 'I have something to say to you, Akanashi. Come with me.' And, leading him to a secret place behind the trees in the garden, he said to him : 'My master has ordered me to choose someone very strong to kill his courtier Shingokeï Dizaki, and I can think of no one better fitted than you for this mission. Go then to Shingokeï's house and kill him. I am sure that my master has an excellent reason for having him destroyed.'

Senpatji asked : 'What is the offence which Shingokeï must expiate ? ' But the minister himself did not know. Then Senpatji said to him : 'I have confidence in your word, yet I should like to hear this order from my master's own lips.' So the minister brought Senpatji before the Lord, who, as Senpatji kneeled before him, said : 'Senpatji, you must kill Shingokeï, as my minister has told you.'

Senpatji returned to his house very sad at having to kill Shingokeï, who was one of his best friends. Nevertheless he went to that man's house and, after a short conversation, killed him, saying: 'It is at the command of my master.'

Shingokeï's slaves tried to seize the murderer; but Senpatji calmed them by saying: 'I have acted on my master's order, and you must obey him.'

The Lord confiscated all Shingokeï's property and his wealth. His widow was inconsolable. She was the daughter of a retired samurai of the neighbouring Province, and had married Shingokeï the year before with customary rites, for Shingokeï and her father were old friends. They loved each other tenderly, and her husband's death stunned her. She wished to die with him and follow him into the other world; but she was pregnant, and could not kill herself because of the child she carried in her womb. So she left the Province, bitterly bewailing her husband's and her own sad destiny. After a long solitary journey full of hardship she came to another very remote Province in the mountains, and decided to live there. Some time after, quite alone and without assistance, she gave birth to a son. She took infinite care of the child, working with her needle to gain a livelihood; for in all the village there was not a single woman who could sew. The two lived thus together in poverty in that place.

Time passed, and the son reached his fourteenth year. His features and his manners were gentle and refined, and he recalled to his mother that cherished husband she had lost. She had kept a Corean harp and two swords fashioned by Kunimune, a celebrated ancient Japanese armourer, which her parents had given her when she left them. When she felt sad she used to play on the harp to distract herself and her dear son. In this manner they lived in their secluded hut.

The destiny of man is surely inconstant and full of surprise. Senpatji Akanashi was banished by his master for some trifling offence; and, after travelling through several Provinces, he settled in a town near the hut in which the mother and son were living. They never met each other, and had no suspicion that they existed at such proximity. But one day Senpatji was invited by his friend Kurobatji Toriyama to hunt birds. On their way back they chanced to pass the widow's cottage, and heard the sound of the Corean harp which the mother was playing. They were charmed by this music and stopped to listen. Slipping through a hole in the hedge, they even peeped through a crack in the bamboo wall. A very beautiful woman of about thirty-five was playing the harp. She seemed to belong to some famous family of the high nobility, and to have disguised herself to live in this wretched hovel. Sitting by her side was her son Shynosuke, studying the writing in a book which his mother had written herself. He was extremely handsome. The interested spectators were surprised to find such distinguished persons in this lonely village. They caused the door to be opened, and stood for some minutes at the entrance to apologise for their intrusion. After a short visit they went away.

Senpatji was struck by the beauty of the young boy; he returned to the hut and became the intimate friend of its inhabitants. Little by little Senpatji and Shynosuke conceived a deep love for each other, and Senpatji took both mother and son with him to his town and there maintained them. In this way a year went peacefully.

Then the mother noticed that Senpatji was very like the man who had killed her husband. One day she questioned him concerning his family and past life; then she became certain that he was the assassin of her husband, the father of her son. Next day she said to the boy: ' Senpatji killed your father before you were born. He was compelled to do so by the command of his master, who was also your father's master; but he is none the less your father's murderer. Kill him, and avenge your father.'

Her son was at first dumb with astonishment.

44

Then he reasoned with his mother : ' Senpatji did not kill my father out of personal enmity. He bore my father no hatred. He could not act otherwise, since the Lord commanded it. He is not really my father's enemy. If you wish to avenge him, it is the Lord Jibudayu whom I ought to kill, not my friend Senpatji. We owe him much gratitude for his kindness. Think, mother : I cannot kill him. We have no right to kill him.'

But his mother was angry, and cried : ' I know that you cannot kill him ; you are too cowardly and soft. If I had known that he was my husband's murderer I should never have accepted his help. I would rather have starved to death than see you form a friendship with him. But I tell you that you are wrong to abandon your revenge because of your love, and, if you do so, you smirch the honour of a samurai. If you are such a coward I no longer know you. I will avenge him myself.'

And, seizing her dagger, she rushed forth. But her son caught her by the sleeve, and said : ' If you are so firmly determined to avenge my father, there is nothing for me to do but obey you. I shall kill him with my own hands. I pray you not to do it yourself, mother. I beg you to be calm.' And he made ready his vengeance.

His love with Senpatji had already lasted for more than two years, and yet he was now compelled to destroy that man to whom he had vowed both affection and assistance for ever. He could not, however, kill him without telling him his reason for doing so. So that evening he called Senpatji to his room, but he was pale and weighed down with sorrow. Senpatji at once perceived this, and said to him : ' Dear Shynosuke, you seem very sad this evening. Are you in trouble? Tell it to me, that I may share it.'

Shynosuke sighed, touched by these gentle words ; and Senpatji again urged him to open his heart. Then Shynosuke confessed to him : ' Oh, what a wretched business is this human life ! I am the son of Shingokeï Dizaki. You know yourself what you did to my father. I am aware that you could not do otherwise, and that you acted at your master's command. But as the son of a samurai I cannot overlook the matter. At that time I was still in my mother's womb. Truly I am sorry to kill you, for you have been good to my mother and myself. I am in great distress.'

Senpatji sighed : ' Alas, it is indeed a strange world ! I never suspected that you were his son. Yes, I killed your father. But I am happy, O Shynosuke, to die at your hands. Come, kill me, and avenge your father.' And he threw away his swords and offered his neck to Shynosuke.

Shynosuke cried : ' No, take your sword and fight with me. I cannot kill you in cold blood, who have been so good to us.' His mother was watching this scene from the next room, and called her son to her, saying : ' I admire both you and Senpatji. Each is a man of honour. Love each other again for this one night. I wish to grant you such an interval. Celebrate your separation, but to-morrow without fail, O Shynosuke, avenge your father.'

Then Shynosuke brought dishes and cups of wine, and the two rejoiced. The mother slept in the next room, and Senpatji and Shynosuke lay down together.

When the woman woke in the morning, they were both silent, lying in the same bed. She called her son : ' Rise up, lazy boy ! ' But there was no answer. She went into the room and turned back the blanket which covered them, and saw that Shynosuke had pierced Senpatji's heart with his sword passed through his own breast and out at his back.

His mother stood there for a long time overwhelmed at the sight of these two lovers' bodies, and then, in her sorrow and distress, killed herself in the same room. Surely a sad and a tragic tale.

7

They Loved Each Other even to Extreme Old Age

THERE WAS A LITTLE SHOP IN A STREET OF the Yanaka district of Yedo, with a narrow bill hung in the doorway which read: 'We have a remedy for superfluous hairs. It is equally good for many other ailments.' Copybooks for students were also sold there; but since these were written by the hand of an old man, no one bought them. A bamboo blind hung between the worn and dirty screens. The trade of that shop was negligible, and the proprietor did not make enough out of it to live by. A graceful pine tree rose above the sloping roof; summer chrysanthemums flourished in the garden, and there was a well of pure water and a pail on the end of a pole. Sometimes birds came and perched on the pail.

The owner of the shop was an old samurai, who had abandoned his career as a samurai when he was still young. He lived on the money he had obtained by the sale of his former garments and his precious family heirlooms. He had only one intimate friend, who was of the same age as himself; and they very often played chess together. His only other companion was a little dog. He had no other visitors, except his few rare customers. Once, at the end of a hot summer day, he removed his clothes, which were soaked with sweat, and took a bath in his garden. His friend wept at the sight of his worn old body, and tenderly caressed the poor bent back. With his voice full of tears he said, as he washed his friend's wrinkled and bony shoulders : 'A certain great Chinese poet said in one of his poems : " A fine young man proudly sang the beauty of his body, admiring himself in a mirror. But that was yesterday. To-day, alas ! he is no more than a poor old man worn out with wrinkles, and his head is covered with grey hair." That is exactly our own story. We have sung together hand in hand without a care when we were young. But now it is only a distant memory and a dream.' Then the two old men joined hands and wept tears of regret for their past, while the hot water in the little tub grew cold.

These two men were samurais who had been born in the Province of Tjikuzen. The younger's name was Mondo Tamashima, and he had been celebrated for the beauty of his face. Many people took him for a young Princess. The elder was called Hayemon Toyoda, and was a skilful marksman. He fell in love with Mondo, who returned his love sincerely. Mondo was sixteen years old and Hayemon nineteen when their love began. They were strongly devoted to each other, and vowed an affection deeper than the sea.

But another samurai loved Mondo. He was jealous of the two friends' love, and contrived all sorts of devices to calumniate them, and tried to separate them by the agency of treacherous persons. But one dark night the two lovers met and killed these persons. Then they fled in a boat and hid themselves for a long time, and finally came to Yedo. There they lived as Guards, concealing their true condition. Mondo was now sixty-three years old, and Hayemon sixty-six; and through all these years their hearts had not changed. They had never taken any interest in a woman. They had been genuine pederasts. Hayemon continued to consider Mondo as his young lover. He arranged his thin hair with his own hands in the style of a page's hair, using much perfumed oil. Mondo's brow was like that of a woman, and he took great care of his person; he polished his nails with aromatic wood, and shaved himself carefully. There is no doubt that these two old men continued their amorous encounters up to an advanced age.

Male love is essentially different from the ordinary love of a man and a woman; and that is why a Prince, even when he has married a beautiful Princess, cannot forget his pages. Woman is a creature of absolutely no importance; but sincere pederastic love is true love. Both of these men detested woman as a vile garden worm. They never associated with their neighbours, and when a near-by husband and wife quarrelled and started breaking the crockery and the doors, these two old men did not try to reconcile them: on the contrary, they encouraged the husband, crying: 'Be brave, O man, and strong! Kill her, beat her to death! Drive her from your house, and take a handsome man instead of her!' They used to shake their fists at the woman, and thought the man feeble and lacking in courage.

In the spring Mount Uyeno is thronged with visitors who come to see the cherry trees loaded with blossom, and at such time people drink excellent wines, and many get drunk. As the folk passed Hayemon's house, he used to distinguish the women's voices from the men's. When he heard men's voices, he ran out in the hope of seeing some beautiful youth: but when he heard women's voices, he shut his door and remained perfectly indifferent.

One day it started to rain, and several women who were making a pleasure party were caught in the shower. They all ran for shelter beneath the eaves of Hayemon's house, and chattered together : ' If we knew who lived here, we could get ourselves invited to tea and rest till the evening ; and perhaps they would lend us umbrellas. They might even invite us to an agreeable supper. It is a great pity that we are not their friends.' One of them, who was older, bolder and less scrupulous than the rest, dared to open the door a little and cast a glance into the house.

Then Hayemon in fury seized a bamboo cane and drove the woman away, crying : ' Get out of here, you vile female ! You witch, you very poisoner, begone ! ' When the terrified woman had run away, he purified the place with salt and clean sand. It is an ancient Japanese custom to spread salt and sand to purify a place which has been polluted. Without doubt there was never in all the great town of Yedo a fiercer enemy of women.

8

A Samurai becomes a Beggar through his Love for a Page

A YOUNG SAMURAI NAMED GUZAYEMON Toyawa lived in a house by himself in his master's palace near Toranomon. One day, being at liberty, he went out for a walk, as he was tired of his bachelor solitude. When young he had been famous for his manly beauty, and had lived in the town of Matsuyama in the Province of South Shikoku ; but he had at length left his former master and come to Yedo. There he was soon engaged by another Lord at the same salary which he had received at Matsuyama. His house was in the Shibuya district.

Mid-spring had come, and the weather was delightful. He went to visit the shrine of the god Tudo at Meguro. Passing by a little waterfall in the temple garden, he saw a beautiful young man. This youth was wearing a large hat decorated with silk and kept in place by a pale blue ribbon : his wide-sleeved robe was as purple as the glory of morning flowers : he carried at his girdle two swords in wonderfully-ornamented scabbards : he was walking at ease carrying a branch of yellow flowers in his hand. His beauty was such that Guzayemon for a moment asked himself if the god Roya had not taken human form, or if a peony had not come to life and was walking in the spring sunlight.

He was fascinated by the young man, who was already accompanied by two shaven courtiers and several servants, and followed him. Guzaye-mon thought that he must be the favourite page of some noble Prince. He was profoundly disturbed, and followed him.

The two shaven courtiers were singing gay songs, for they were a little drunk. The young boy went towards a palace near the shrine of Koroku, and entered it by a door crowned with violet paulownia leaves. Guzayemon asked a Guard what this palace might be, and learned that the young man's name was Shyume Oku-yama, the favourite page of his master.

Guzayemon dreamed of the boy all night. Next day he stood before the palace door, hoping to see the page ; but in vain. Returning to his house, he could not keep his mind on his work. He pretended to be ill, and resigned from his service. He then went to live in a little house in a street in the Kojimachi district. Since his time was all his own, he walked every day before the palace door, from the twenty-third of May till the month of October ; but he never saw the young man again. He had no means of sending him a love-letter, and therefore suffered cruelly from his passion by day and by night.

Then the young page's master received permission from the Shyôgun to return to his own country, and the twenty-fifth day was fixed for his departure. Guzayemon decided to follow the page; so he sold all the furniture of his house, shut it up, and paid his debts to the grocer, the fishmonger and the wine merchant; he dismissed his young servant, and followed the train of the Lord.

The train stopped for their first night in the town of Kanayawa, and next day took up their quarters at Oysso. That evening the page went out in a litter to visit historic Shigitatsusawa. He opened the door of his litter a trifle and murmured the famous poem which Saïgyô, the Buddhist priest, had written concerning that palace:

Although I have renounced all human emotion
As a priest of Buddha,
I am seized with deep sadness
When I find myself here at Shigitatsusawa
On an Autumn evening.

Guzayemon could only behold his love from a distance; yet the other also perceived him, and their looks crossed. But they were immediately separated, and Guzayemon did not see the

page again until a day when they were going
along a rocky road at the summit of Mount
Utsunoyama. Guzayemon was standing behind
a big rock at the side of the road, and threw a
glance into the young man's litter; then, in
spite of himself, he began to weep with emotion.
The young man turned his gracious face to
him, and Guzayemon became more than ever
inflamed.

He did not see his page again before they
reached the town of Tsuyama in the Province
of Mimasaka, and there he caught but a bare
glimpse of him. That was his last chance, for
soon the Lord arrived safely in the Province of
Yezumo. There Guzayemon became a labourer
to gain his food, for he had spent all his money
during the long journey from Yedo to
Yezumo.

In the following year the Lord again set out for
Yedo, to pay his court to the Shyôgun in
April. Guzayemon followed in his train a
second time; but he only beheld the page thrice
during the whole journey: once in the ferry at
Kuwana, the second time on the steep hill of
Shihomizaki, and the last time in the grove of
Suzuga, quite close to Yedo. Then the Lord
remained for a whole year at Yedo.

Guzayemon went every day to the palace in the
hope of seeing his love. With the life that he

was leading, all his refinement and distinguished appearance had gone from him. He was haggard and miserable. No one could have discerned in him a fallen samurai, whose beauty had once been famous. His health was also affected.

Next year he again followed the Lord from Yedo to his Province. He looked like a beggar, so greatly had he suffered. His clothes had more than one hole in them, and his sleeves were torn. But he kept his two swords, which are the soul of a samurai.

In the outskirts of a town called Kanaya he saw the page's litter. And Shyume saw Guzayemon from his litter, and understood that Guzayemon loved him. He was deeply touched by such an attachment, and wished to speak to him. So he descended from his litter, while the train stopped for a short time on Mount Sayono Nakayama, and stood waiting for Guzayemon to approach. But Guzayemon was too far off to come near him, and they saw each other no more on that occasion. Guzayemon did not indeed behold him again during the whole of that journey, though he did not cease to think of him.

His feet were worn and bleeding from his long walking ; he had no more money, and ended by becoming a beggar by the roadside. But he

57

clung desperately to his miserable life. He pro-
tected his body from rain, snow and wind with
a thin reed hat and a garment of woven grass.
He shivered when it blew cold. During the
day he stayed in a vile thatched hut in a field,
and at evening, when Shyume returned home to
his master's palace, stood near the palace door
and consoled himself by watching the dear lad
from a distance.

One rainy evening Shyume called his servant,
Kuzayemon, because he felt lonely and very
bored after his day's service, and said to him :
' I was born of a family of samurai, and I have
not yet killed a living man with my sword.
Yet I must have practice in case of a battle. I
cannot be a good warrior if I have no exercise
in the art of killing. Kuzayemon, I wish to try
to kill a living man this evening,'

His servant rebuked him : ' Dear master, you
are an excellent swordsman, and very expert
with your weapon. You are not inferior to any
of the courtiers of this company. You have
nothing to fear in this matter, nothing at all.
Heaven will punish you if you kill a living man
without sufficient reason, merely from caprice.
I beg you to wait for a more serious occasion to
exercise your skill.'

Shyume explained to him : ' I do not wish to
kill an honourable man, dear Kuzayemon.

Over there by the street gutter there is a beggar, who seems entirely wretched. He cannot love his life. Ask him to give me his life, after I have satisfied all his desires.'

The servant answered : ' Even in that miserable state he will not wish to die.' Yet he went up to the beggar and said : ' Dear friend, I have a favour to beg of you. This human life is, as you know, but a vain thing. It is also as uncertain as one of this evening's showers. We cannot know how long it may last and when it will cease. You have come to a truly lamentable condition, and I think that life does not offer you much pleasure. My young master has commanded me to ask if you would be willing to give him your life to die by his sword, because he wishes to practise his weapons upon a living person. But, before killing you, he will allow you to continue for thirty days, during which time he will cause you to live splendidly. He will engage a priest to perform a fine funeral for you also. What do you think of this ? '

The beggar answered : ' I know that I shall not live until next Spring, and every night I suffer because of the cold air. I have no friends, and none will care what has become of me. I am quite ready to be killed by your master.'

The servant then led him to Shyume, support-
ing his weak and trembling body with his
hands, and told of the success of his mission.
They first made the man take a bath to wash
himself; then they gave him clean clothes and
a servant's room. They fed him for ten days
on the most delicious dishes, according to his
desire. On the appointed evening, when it
was already late, he was led to a secluded part
of Shyume's garden.

Shyume looked at his pale, haggard face, and
asked : ' Are you really willing to make me this
present of your life ? '

The beggar stretched out his neck to receive the
mortal wound, saying : ' I am quite ready,
Lord. Cut off my head.' Shyume raised his
skirt, so as to be more free in his movement,
and went up to the other, brandishing his
sword. He struck him with it, but it did not
wound him at all ; for it was quite without an
edge. The beggar and the servant were aston-
ished at this. But Shyume dismissed all his
attendants and shut the gate of the garden. He
was now alone with Guzayemon, whom he led
into his apartment, saying : ' I recognise your
face : you must have been a samurai.' But the
beggar denied it.

Shyume insisted : ' You are lying. I know
that you love me passionately. Open your

heart to me, and do not hide your thought. If you keep your secret now, when will you tell it ; and to whom, if not to me ? Or am I mistaken in thinking that you love me ? '

The beggar drew from his bosom a little packet wrapped in bamboo bark, and opened it. From it he took a purse of gold silk which he offered to Shyume, saying with tears : ' My heart is locked in that.' Shyume unfastened the purse, and took out sixty leaves of thin paper on which Guzayemon had written the story of his love, from the first day that he saw Shyume near the shrine of the god Tudo, up to that last day when he had waited before the door.

Shyume read five of the leaves, and then replaced them in the purse, putting the latter in his pocket. He summoned his servants and ordered them to guard Guzayemon. Next morning he went to the Lord and said : ' Lord, a man is madly in love with me, and I cannot find the cruelty to reject him. But if I accept his love, I disobey you, Lord, and show myself ungrateful towards you. I do not know what to do. I have no idea. Lord, I pray you to kill me with your sword and free me from my dilemma.'

The Lord asked him for the details of this story, and Shyume gave him the papers written by Guzayemon, which the Lord read secretly in his room. Then he summoned Shyume and told him to return home and await his orders, until he should have weighed his decision. Shyume answered : ' My lover is in my house, and if you send me back I shall love him. Let me die here by Hara-kiri.'

After a little thought the Lord sentenced Shyume to be confined in his own house, whereupon Shyume quickly returned home and made Guzayemon assume the dress of a true samurai, and gave him two swords. Shyume and Guzayemon then loved each other madly and passionately, expecting every minute to be condemned to death by command of their master. This ardent love, at the price of life itself, was daring and audacious. But after twenty days the Lord pardoned Shyume, and gave him twenty suits of man's clothing and much money, saying to him : ' Send your samurai back to Yedo.'

Shyume was very grateful for his Lord's kindness and generosity. Without delaying until next day, he made ready for Guzayemon's departure.

When he reached the Province of Yedo, Guzayemon sent back all Shyume's men who had accompanied him. Instead of going to Yedo, he climbed up the high mountain of Katsororaju, in the Province of Yamato, and there lived

From the Japanese

as a hermit, remaining on the mountain and
seeing no one. He called himself Mugento, the
priest of dream. He cut off his hair. He
spent all his days watching the cool
springs flow from the rocks
beside his dwelling.

9

An Actor loved his Patron, even as a Flint Seller

THERE WAS ONCE A CELEBRATED FEMALE-character-actor named Sennojyo. He had made his first appearance on the stage at the age of fourteen, and at forty-two years of age was still so popular that people loved to see him portray feminine characters. His greatest success was in the drama called *While going toward Kawashi to an assignation*, which was performed for three years at Yedo.

But one autumn an epidemic disease of the spinal marrow broke out in Yedo, and to this Sennojyo fell a victim. His back grew bent and deformed, and he altogether lost his grace of body. But he was gifted with high talent and intelligence, and did not lose his popularity because of his disease. Many employers even found it difficult to secure him for their comedies ; for, when he was a little drunk, his cheeks became rosy, giving him such charm that many men fell in love with him. Several well-known priests lost their heads about him, and spent so much money to have him that they were obliged to sell the precious relics of their temples to gain an interview. Some of these were even so mad as to sell the holy trees of the sacred forests, for which they were driven from their temples and became beggars. Many clerks also spent their employers' money to see Sennojyo privately, and ruined their masters.

Once, when he was still young, Sennojyo took his diary from a little private chest. Its title was *My experiences with many men*, and it was a very interesting record. He started to read it through. He had noted down in it all his impressions, from the very first day, of widely different people. Sometimes he would go to a samurai's room. By the mere caress of his hand he would soothe a demon in an angry man. He would make men of refinement or priests even out of farmers. In a word, he had treated each of his different patrons in the way most suitable to him. He shut the diary with a smile. But suddenly he thought of one of his patrons who had been most devoted to him. Sennojyo did not know where this man was. That evening a violent gale blew up, and snow began to fall. The mountains to the north of Kyoto were already white. A wretched-looking man was standing under the Gojyo bridge. He lived on the bank of the river Kamo, and there he slept during the night. In the morning he gathered pebbles from the river Kurama and sold them in Kyoto for gun flints. Those that he had been unable to sell he threw away in the evening. His life under this bridge was very miserable.

He had formerly been one of the rich men of the Province of Owari. He had been given over to male love. He had written a book in four volumes, called *A Collection of Stories Pure as Crystal,* in which he had recorded in every detail everything that he knew of any of Sennojyo's actions and gestures. In it he mentioned even such a trifling matter as a black mole on the actor's back. He had loved Sennojyo with all his heart from the first day the latter had appeared upon the stage ; but some time afterwards he had wearied of all earthly joys and had hidden himself away from society.

Sennojyo had been greatly grieved at not being able to find this man again, and always bitterly regretted his disappearance. Someone informed him that his patron was living miserably on the bank of the Kamo, and he burst into tears, saying : ' Truly the destiny of man is variable. If he had let me know of his situation, I should not have left him in such misery. I have written him many letters to his house in Owari, but he has never answered me. I sorrowfully thought he had forgotten me, as frequently happens with us poor actors.'

66

From the Japanese

That night Sennojyo received his patrons in the tea-house with the greatest cordiality; but at dawn he went to the bank of the river Kamo to look for his former patron. He went alone, without a servant, along the gritty and pebbly river bank, with the river flowing at his side. At last he reached the bridge, and called: 'Samboku, my dear Owari patron!' But no one answered him. It was the twenty-fourth of November, and not yet very light; therefore he could not distinguish the faces of the wretched men lying under the bridge. There were many beggars and vagabonds there.

Then he remembered that his patron had a little scar on his neck; so he started to examine all the sleepers closely, and after a long search found his man. 'You are cruel,' he said. 'I have kept calling you, and you never answered.' And he wept for pity and joy at finding his old lover again, and chatted with him a little of past days and of their former love. The morning air was fresh, and to warm the two of them Sennojyo poured out the wine which he had brought, and they both drank. When the sky grew light in the East he could distinguish his old lover's features. He had lost all refinement, and Sennojyo was very sorry for this. He tenderly caressed the scurfed feet, and lay down with the old man under the bridge.

67

Day came and people began to pass over the bridge; and the time came for the announcement of the theatre programme. Sennojyo was obliged to retire secretly, for he could not stay there in the sight of all. He said to the old man: 'I beg you to wait for me here this evening. I shall come and take you back to my house with me.' But the old man had no wish to accept such a proposal. This meeting with his former lover had, in fact, troubled him. He wished to continue in his simple and serene obscurity. Therefore he disappeared.

Sennojyo sought him through all Kyoto, but in vain. He collected all the gun flints that his lover had left behind, and made a tomb of them among the bamboos, in a corner of the field of Nii-Kamano at Higashiyama. His lover's favourite tree had been the violet paulownia, so he planted one beside the tomb. He engaged a priest, who lived in a little hut near the field, to pray for his lover's and his own soul. People named this tomb, 'The new tomb of love.'

10

*Letter from a Buddhist Priest telling
his Friend that his Lover comes
to him*

DEAR FRIEND IN THE TEACHING OF BUDDHA:
The cherry trees in flower at Kyoto so
troubled me that I left the capital laſt spring. I
send you this letter by a man who is going to
visit the city. I hope that you are zealous in
our religion at your temple, and without dis-
turbance.

My hut muſt have become the resort of mice
and rats since it has been unoccupied ; though
there is not a single piece of fish left there for
such gueſts to enjoy. You may laugh at my
poverty, dear friend. No one will regret the
chrysanthemums when they fade in my garden.
But if by chance you should be passing near my
hut, enter, and, since I have given you the key,
let the weary passers-by come in. I buried
some nuts and potatoes under the north door :
use them, for otherwise they will be spoiled.
Takenaka sent me these provisions, and I do
not like to waſte them.

And now I shall speak to you of myself. As
you know, my eternal and incurable weakness
is to fall in love with some pretty boy ; and I
confess to you that I have an affair here with

an entrancing lad, and I hesitate to return to Kyoto.

Last year, on leaving the capital, I went to my friend at Okayama in the Province of Bizen. He received me very hospitably, but I quickly grew weary there; so I went by boat to the Province of Higo, where I have a friend who is a poet and a priest of the temple of Kiyomasa, and I lived with him.

One evening I was in his wonderful garden, enjoying the fresh breeze after a hot day. An artificial stream flowed between fanciful rocks and grass-covered hillocks which had been built up there. The effect was as the dwelling of some mountain hermit, delighting in spiritual beauty and the pure pleasures of the soul. The faint song of a cuckoo rose from the density of the mighty pines behind the temple, so poignantly pure that I thought I had never heard such beautiful song in Kyoto. I thought that a cuckoo, singing in the evening in so sacred a place as the temple of Kiyomasa, would make a fitting subject for a poem. I began to compose a poem in my head, and was thinking out the rhymes and the arrangement of the syllables.

Then there came out of the temple the whole of the High Priest's train. Amongst them walked a very beautiful page, about sixteen years old,

70

so lovely that I thought I had never seen such charm and elegance even in the flowering capital. I was indeed surprised to see so beautiful a page in such a remote district as the Western Province of Higo. I was greatly troubled by him. Formerly I had become very weary of the luxurious and artificial life of our capital; but at that moment, in this distant country, I felt a temptation which disturbed all the peace of my spirit. My soul was quite thrown into confusion, and my heart began to beat violently with desire. When the High Priest left the temple after his prayer, I watched the page from behind a screen, and my love grew with each minute. I asked my friend who this beautiful page was, and he told me that he was the second son of a noble family, whose parents had entrusted him to the High Priest because he wished to become a priest and to renounce the pleasures of this world.

My love became so violent that it seemed to me that my soul was breaking into a thousand pieces; and it was, indeed, torn. I lost my calm, and in vain gravely reproached myself. I could not forget this beautiful young man. At last in despair, without caring what my friend thought, I wrote the page a love-letter, pleading the cause of my despairing soul. I hoped to gain a little peace if he should only know of my love, without going nearly so far as to return it.

This is what I wrote :

' DEAR AND ROYAL LORD,

' I saw you yesterday evening when you were crossing the garden in the High Priest's train, and was moved by your beauty. You are so lovely that the most famous beauties of China, such as Taitjio and Token, the fairest young men there, or Hi or the Empress Yo cannot excel you. I am a priest, but, alas ! I have also the passions of a man, and I confess that I love you with all my being. Lord, I am a humble and insignificant priest, passing through this Province : you are of a noble family. To aspire to your love is, for me, as impossible and unfeasible as to climb up a ladder to heaven. I admit that it is impudent of me even to love you ; but I write to you because I hope to win some satisfaction and contentment by simply letting you know that I do so. I am like a fly in a spider's web, I am helpless. I bring you my heart in these clumsy words.

' Since I saw you my heart has not ceased to beat violently. When I am alone, flaming tears run down my cheeks. I am in actual agony ; and my words in this letter are all confused. Your face and your whole person are so refined and elegant. I have heard it said that you are the most splendid flower of the Western Provinces ; but to me you seem the most precious jewel in the universe. For indeed your beauty exceeds all the flowers of the world. For me, you are as princely a beauty as the Empress Seishi, or the celebrated poetess Komachi, or the young Yukihira* or the new-born Narihira. I cannot forget you even in my sleep ; and when I awake I am excruciated. I have prayed the god Fuyisaki to have pity on my unhappy love. I wish to drown myself in the river Kikutji, to put an end to my pain. I am ready to sacrifice my life for one evening's love with you. One evening of love with you is more precious than a thousand years of life. I shall gladly do all that you command me. I would rather have half an hour's life than drag out mere miserable existence for a hundred years. From morning to evening, by day and by night, your face does not leave me, and I endure a thousand deaths for love of you. I am wretched. I am cursed by a cruel Karma.'

But, my dear friend, I am blessed rather than cursed. He has read my letter and sent me such a kind answer. Oh, how tender and sympathetic he is ! I am happy and contented ; I am the happiest man under the sun. I cannot speak enough of his kindness, for he is truly good. That is all that I can say now. Presently, as soon as he finds an opportunity, he is coming to spend a whole evening with me. All that troubles me is that the day is not yet fixed. I know that this waiting for the day is an agony which all lovers have to endure ; and I comfort myself by telling myself so.

I wish I could show you this noble young man. His name is Aineme Okayima. When he comes to see me, we shall drink wine together and have a pleasant conversation by ourselves. I should like the night to last for ever, and that the dawn should never come to put an end to our meeting. This is all that I can tell you at present : there is nothing further. I hope to be calmer and more balanced after seeing him.

Till then, farewell, dear comrade,

From your far-distant friend.

At Last Rewarded for his Constancy

WHEN HIDEYOSHI RULED JAPAN AFTER THE Ashikaya dynasty had died out, he lived at Fushimi ; and all the Lords and Princes of all the Provinces of Japan were obliged to live near him.

At that time the Lord of the Province of Izumi had a page named Inosuke Murola who was most beautiful and very brave. He was as graceful and delicate as the cherry flower, but his soul was as fearless as the god of war. At first sight you would have taken him for a charming Princess of royal blood. The Lord preferred him to all his other pages. But another page was jealous of the favours shown to Inosuke, and made a completely false and outrageous accusation against him, which he wrote on paper and left in the hall of the palace. The overseer of the palace found the paper and took it to his master, since it was his duty to report even the most insignificant thing to him ; and the Lord was furious at his favourite's scandalous behaviour. He was so angry that he dismissed Inosuke from his service, without inquiring whether the accusation were well founded, and banished him from Fushimi without giving him any reason for his disgrace.

He ordered his courtiers to keep a strict watch over him, and not to let him stir one step from his house. Inosuke, the victim of false testimony, was confined in a little cottage with his old mother, and was strictly guarded. The doors were locked, and not even his relatives were allowed to come to see him.

His mother and he were completely ignorant of the cause of their disgrace ; therefore Inosuke could not commit Hara-kiri, which would otherwise have been the only expedient for a samurai reduced to such a pass. All the servants, anxious for their own interest, abandoned him one after another, fearing to place themselves in the wrong by remaining with a samurai disgraced.

Then came times of great hardship for Inosuke and his mother. Grieving for her son's sorrow, she cooked his meals, a thing which she had never done. And her son was pained to see his mother compelled to such base and menial labour. He used to go and fetch water from a well in the garden, and help her in the kitchen. In this miserable manner they dragged on their lives. The days passed, and the months ; even the years went by and the Spring seasons returned. Mother and son were astonished by the quick passage of time. Then their means of existence grew scant, and they sold their last

possessions. At last they were at the end of
their resources.

One evening the mother said despairingly to her
son : ' Dear Inosuke, we have nothing more to
live on, and, indeed, to continue this existence
is merely to prolong our suffering. I think that
it is better to die than to remain in such a
pitiable state. If I do not die a beautiful death
by committing suicide, it is no shame; for I am
an old woman. But you are a young samurai,
and you must pass honourably. Be brave,
my son, and go first. I shall follow you
straightway.'

Inosuke calmly answered : ' Yes, mother.' He
did up his hair, bared his breast, and serenely sat
down on a mat. He was already holding the
knife in his hand and preparing to kill himself,
when there crept into the room a little dog
which seemed to belong to some good family.
It was white with some black spots, and had a
collar with a little bell. Tied to its neck were
two packets wrapped in paper. It wagged its
tail very familiarly, and went up to Inosuke as
if it wanted to speak to him.

The astonished mother untied the packets and
opened them. One contained some provisions,
and a note on which was written this sentence :
' It is easy to die.' In the other packet were
some comforts and another note with this

sentence : ' But it is more difficult to live for honour's sake.'

In this manner someone had sent them help just as they were despairing. Mother and son wondered who in the world this person could have been who wished them well. Someone at least knew of the injustice of their disgrace. They resolved to live a little longer, and delayed their death. They caressed the dog, who was very pleased with this and went out by a hole in the wall. After that, the faithful little beast came every morning and evening, bringing round his neck something for their subsistence.

Two years passed in this way, and it was now five since the Lord had exiled them and confined them to their cottage. Inosuke was grieving to death, and indeed fell ill ; but a kindly Heaven was watching over them. The Lord at last relented and delivered them from this long disgrace. Inosuke thanked him, and asked the reason for his punishment. The Lord showed him the paper telling of his scandalous conduct, and Inosuke at once guessed that another page, named Naminojyo Toyura, had plotted to denounce him to his master because he was jealous of him, and that he who had written the false and outrageous accusation was a certain fencing master of the people, named Kenpatji Iwasaka.

Both of these men were put to a cruel death. The Lord regretted that he had punished Inosuke so long and so unjustly, and made him a samurai and Keeper of the Seals. Thus Inosuke's honour was ensured, and the people loved and honoured him more than before.

He then returned to his Province and called together all his relatives, to ask them who had been the charitable person who had sent the dog to comfort him and his mother when they were in despair. But it was none of them; and Inosuke continued to search for his benefactor. One day, as he was walking in the quarter of the samurai, he saw the dog which had visited him sleeping in front of the door of a house. A passer-by told him that this was the house of Shibei Okazaki, one of the Lord's chief officers. Then Inosuke remembered that Shibei had at one time vowed an ardent love for him. Inosuke had not forgotten him, even when he was loved by his Lord, and he thought: 'I must never forget what he did for me during my long disgrace. I could not repay, even by giving my life for him. Should anything happen to him, I swear upon my honour as a samurai that I shall help him with my death.'

That evening Inosuke sent for Shibei, and, when the latter arrived, thanked him with tears. After his mother had retired to her room, Inosuke and Shibei had a very pleasant and cordial conversation. Inosuke asked how the dog had known the house and the hole to come in by, and Shibei answered : 'When you were in this Province with your master, I could not restrain my love for you, and used to walk before your house nearly every night. But I dared not see you, because you were our Lord's favourite. I only stood outside and tried to satisfy my burning love by the sight of you or the sound of your voice. My dog followed me every night, and thus he learned to know your house, and I was able to send him to help you.'

Inosuke blushed with pleasure at Shibei's devotion, and confessed : 'It grieves me much that I was unable to return your love at that time ; but my Lord loved me. Now I am free to love you ; but I am no longer the pretty page I was when you cared for me so deeply. I am now a faded flower. But why regret the past ? I have become a samurai, and am no longer a page ; but I have the same heart for you. Love me, if you can feel the same ardency as before. I shall be happy to be loved by you.'

And Inosuke put on his old page's dress with long sleeves, although it was not suitable for a grown man, for he wished to recall past days. They spent the night together in his room, and in their love murmurings Inosuke said to Shibei :

80

From the Japanese

' I am only twenty-one years old,' although he was really twenty-two. A samurai ought never to dissemble, but Inosuke must be excused for his lie, since he was truly in love with his former admirer and could not tell the truth about his age. Even a brave and valiant samurai grows weak when he loves; for love is the greatest power of all and governs this world.

12

He Rids himself of his Foes with the Help of his Lover

EVERY YEAR THE TREES ARE COVERED WITH blossom as in the years before; but man cannot keep the blossom of his youth. The beauty of boys will vanish when they become men, and when the lock of hair is cut from their foreheads, and they are clothed in short-sleeved robes. The love of boys is, therefore, but a passing dream.

Jinnosuke Kasuda, the second son of a courtier of the Lord of the Province of Izumo, was a beautiful boy. He was an excellent swordsman and had a profound knowledge of classical literature; many men were attracted by his beauty. When they assembled round the shrine of Ooyashiro they spoke of him, and were agreed that there was no more beautiful boy in all the Provinces of Japan. But Jinnosuke had already plighted his troth to one of the Lord's courtiers, and his lover's name was Gonkuro Moriwaki, an excellent samurai of some twenty-eight years of age. He had fallen in love with Jinnosuke when the latter was only thirteen years old.

He had first made the acquaintance of Dengoro, Jinnosuke's servant, and, to prevent people

talking, had put his love-letter into the mouth of a great fish, and sent it thus to Dengoro. Next morning, when Dengoro was doing his master's hair and Jinnosuke seemed to be in a good humour, Dengoro gave him the letter and told him how much Gonkuro suffered for love of him.

Without opening the letter, Jinnosuke rapidly wrote an answer to Gonkuro and said to his servant: 'It is very hard to wait when one is in love; take this letter at once to Gonkuro.' 'You are indeed worthy to be adored, master,' said the servant, and ran to Gonkuro's house, to give him the letter, telling him that his master wished him well. Gonkuro, with tears of joy, read the letter, which said: 'Your sincere love fills me with gratitude. My servant has told me this morning that you are suffering because of me. I also am amorous of you. Let us be lovers from this day forth, without caring what people think.' That is how the two samurai began to be in love with each other, in the summer of Jinnosuke's fourteenth year.

They kept their love a secret, and no one suspected it, although it lasted until the autumn of Jinnosuke's sixteenth year. But at that time an official samurai of small nobility, named Ibeï Hanzawa, fell in love with Jinnosuke and sent him several love-letters by his servant, Suizayemon ; all of which Jinnosuke returned without reading them. This exasperated Ibeï, and he wrote Jinnosuke a furious letter : 'You have scorned my love simply because I am a samurai of low position. I am sure that you have a lover. Tell me who he is. If you refuse to impart his name, I shall fight with you wherever I meet you, to avenge my honour as a samurai ; for you have insulted it.' He could easily have died from pride and spleen. Jinnosuke told the whole story to Gonkuro, although he had till then kept silent about it so as not to trouble his friend to little purpose. He wanted to warn his dear Gonkuro. Now the latter was older and more cautious than Jinnosuke, and advised him : 'You ought not to have despised his love, although he is a man of mean condition. We can only love each other because we are alive ; let us not waste our life unprofitably. Be more amiable to Ibeï, and write him a kind letter to appease him, Jinnosuke.' But this proposal made Jinnosuke furious, and he answered with bloodshot eyes : 'I would reject the love even of my Lord, for it is to you that I have pledged my passion.' He was so angry that he would have killed Gonkuro on the spot ; but he calmed himself and resolved to kill Gonkuro after having got rid of Ibeï. He said farewell to Gonkuro as usual, and returned home. Then he wrote to Ibeï : ' To-night there is no moon. Come this evening to the pine-tree-field of the god Teujin, and fight a duel with me because of your grievance. I will await you there.' Then, after greeting his parents, he retired to his room and wrote several farewell letters to his friends and relations. He also wrote a letter of reproach to Gonkuro, in which he said :

' I pledged my love to you for life, and was ready to defend that love with that life, against every obstacle. I am not afraid of this quarrel with Ibeï. I am going to meet him this evening in the pine-tree-field of the god Teujin. If you think of our love years, you will not hesitate to come and die with me. I have much with which to reproach you and, if I cannot tell these things, I feel that I shall not die peacefully. Therefore I wish to tabulate them in this farewell letter.

' The distance between your house and mine is too great. I have traversed that long road three hundred and twenty-seven times during the three years in which our love has lasted ; and every evening I encountered some kind of obstacle or difficulty. I had to hide myself from vigilant people, from guards and watchmen. Often I had to disguise myself as a servant, as an adult with a long lantern. At other times I have travestied myself as a priest. It was not easy for me to perform such humiliating actions, although you may not think so very much of them.

' Last year, on the twentieth of November, my mother lingered in my room and I could not come. I was impatient to see you, for life is so uncertain that we do not know whether we shall live till the morrow, and if I could not see you on that night, perhaps I should never see you again. Therefore, in spite of my disordered dress and the late hour, I managed to come out and creep as far as your house. You heard, by the little noise I made, that I was under the window of your room. You were speaking to someone inside, and there was a light in your room. But, as soon as you heard my step, you put out the light and stopped talking. You were cruel to me then. I should like to know who was the person to whom you were talking on that evening.

' Last spring I wrote, without taking much trouble, the famous poem, " My sleeves are ever wet with tears, for my love is hopeless," on the back of a fan painted with flowers by the celebrated Uneme Kano. You gave me great pleasure by your compliment: " A lover in pain would easily pass the summer with this fan." And you also wrote underneath the poem : " He who inscribed this is waiting his lover." But you gave the fan to your servant Kitjisuke.

'You had a lark which you bought from Jiubeï the bird-seller. You loved it very much, and when I asked you to give it to me, you refused. But later you gave it to Syohatji Kitamura, the prettiest boy of all our company. I am very jealous because of that.

'On the eleventh of last April, the whole country was called together on horseback by the Lord. Tarozayemon Setsubara then detained me and said : "Your skirt is spotted with mud." And he brushed it. You were just behind me, but pretended to be unconcerned. You even laughed at me with Tarozayemon, instead of drawing my attention to the splashes. I think that you did not act well in this, since you had been my lover for so many years.

'On the eighteenth of May I stayed talking to Kanya Osasawara late in the evening, and you were very angry about it. But, as I explained to you then, I had gone to him with my companions Magosaburo and Tomoya Matsubara for our singing lesson. Kanya is too young to have a love affair with me. Magosaburo is my own age. You know Tomoya well. Even if we were to meet every evening, there could be no scandal or amorous association between us. But you always suspected me, and have made frequent insinuations concerning that affair, which have caused me much suffering. Even to-day I cannot forget my sorrow at your unreasonable suspicion.

' Often, after our meetings, you could have accompanied me nearly home ; but you always turned back at the house of Sodayon Murase. Only twice during all our long love have you come the full way with me, as far as my house. I am sure that, if I had really been your true love, you would have borne me company at least beyond the field where the tigers and wolves can be heard howling.

' I have many other things with which to reproach you, but am feeling infinitely sad. And even now I cannot help loving you. I do nothing but weep for my unhappy passion. I beg you to pray, only just once, for the safety of my soul after my death. This world is vain and uncertain ; its contents are but a dream ! I will finish my farewell letter with a poem :

> ' *The morning flowers were born in their beauty.*
> *But the wind rose and carried them away*
> *Even before night.*

' I have still much to write, but evening is drawing near, and I must cease. To my dear Gonkuro from his Jinnosuke. May 26th, in the seventh year of Kuanbun (A.D. 1667).'

He sealed the letter and gave it to his servant, Dengoro, saying : ' Take this letter to Gonkuro this evening when it is dark.' And, as soon as twilight came, he went to the place fixed for the duel. He dressed himself sumptuously, for he thought that it would be his very last costuming. His under-garments were of white silk, and his over-garment was purple with cherry blossoms embroidered on the hips. His emblem was the Jinko,* and his sleeves were long, as they were worn by pages. He carried two swords of Tadoyoshi Hizen in a grey girdle.

The pine-tree-field of the god Teujin was two miles from the town. Jinnosuke sat down on a moss-covered stone opposite a big camphor tree, and waited for his antagonist. As the darkness grew and the shapes of things became dim, Gonkuro arrived out of breath, crying : ' Are you there, Jinnosuke ? ' Jinnosuke answered coldly : ' No one so base is a friend of mine.' Gonkuro began to weep, and said : ' I do not try to excuse myself. I shall tell you all my heart when we are in another world, Jinnosuke. Only then will you know me.'

But Jinnosuke answered icily : ' I have no need of your help. I am strong enough to fight alone.' While they were thus becoming heated, Ibeï Hanzawa arrived, seconded by sixteen

samurai of very vulgar appearance. They
meant to fight fiercely, with no thought for
their lives. Jinnosuke killed two of them,
while Gonkuro struck down four. Seven others
were seriously wounded, the rest fled in terror,
and Ibeï was killed in single combat. Gon-
kuro's servant, Hitjisuke, died defending his
master. Gonkuro had a slight wound on the
forehead, and Jinnosuke was also stricken in the
left shoulder. The two samurai remained con-
querors. There was a little Buddhist temple
called Yeianji quite close, to which Gonkuro
and Jinnosuke walked, and there asked the
priest to bury them, after they had killed them-
selves by Hara-kiri. But the priest dissuaded
them, saying : ' You have both behaved very
honourably in this duel. You ought first to
report the matter to the Lord's advisers and
inspectors ; and you would do better to die
publicly. Then your honour and glory will
endure for ever.'
He persuaded them to follow his advice, and
they obeyed him. Then the priest hurried in
person to the office of the police, and himself
reported the matter. The Lord, through his
inspector, ordered these young men to await
their punishment. They were imprisoned and
guarded during the night, and the Lord ordered
their wounds to be tended. The accomplices

of Ibeï were condemned to death ; and the cowards who had fled were later found and executed.

Jinnosuke had really broken the law by his action. But his father was a very loyal and devoted courtier ; and also Jinnosuke had always done his duty faithfully. In the duel he had given proof of great courage and valour by fighting against so many assailants. The Lord thought that he deserved admiration rather than punishment. Therefore he was acquitted, and Gonkuro also obtained pardon. They were both ordered to leave their official service from the fifteenth of the month.

The priest buried Ibeï and his companions with considerable piety. When Jinnosuke was examined, it was seen that his left sleeve had been cut off, and that his robe was stained with the blood which he had lost. But he did not specially suffer from his wounds, although he had more than twenty-seven of them on his body. He was greatly admired for his courage and endurance.

13

Love long Concealed

FOLLOWING A DISPUTE WITH THE COUN-
sellor of the Lord of the Province of Osumi,
the samurai Jiuzayemon Fatjibana retired from
official life. He lived very comfortably with his
wife and son in a remote village. His son,
Tamanosuke, was at that time fifteen years old,
and so beautiful that people thought it a pity to
leave him hidden in this remote village, and not
to make him a well-known samurai in some
large town.

But when Jiuzayemon thought that his son was
old enough to serve a Prince as a page, he sent
him to the capital, Yedo. He also caused his
servant, Kakubeï Kanazawa, to accompany him.
This man had served him for many years, and
was fifty years old and had great experience of
life. Before leaving him, his father gave his son
some good advice, telling him to conduct
himself bravely and to defend his honour to
the death.

But his mother whispered for a moment with
Kakubeï, asking him to guard and protect her
son, and ended by saying: ' I beg you to take
particular care of my son, especially in this
matter.'

When Tamanosuke and Kakubeï were some

distance from the house, Tamanosuke asked :
' Did not my mother tell you not to deliver
love-letters to me if a samurai should send me
one ? But if you refuse to oblige a man who
sends me love-letters, you will act heartlessly.
You will be a cruel man. I want to be loved by
some great samurai, since that is one of the best
things in this life of ours. If no one loves me,
I shall hate my beautiful face. Once in Great
China, a prevalent poet of the Province of
Yoshu said in one of his poems, speaking of a
young boy : "A cruel youth without a heart."
I wish you to feel sympathy for pederasty, O
Kakubeï.'

Kakubeï answered : ' But of course, young
master ! If everybody were as scrupulous as
your mother, such a thing as honourable love
between samurai would not exist. I shall act
quite in accordance with your wishes.' And
they laughed together.

After a long and troublesome journey they at
last reached Yedo. Tamanosuke was presented
by a friend of his father's to the Prince of the
Province of Aezu, who was charmed with him
and immediately engaged him as a page, and
took him to the Province of Aezu with him.
Tamanosuke was greatly attached to this Lord,
and very polite to the other courtiers, of whom
this Lord made him his favourite. Compared

with Tamanosuke's beauty, all the other pages were as flowers hidden behind a fence from the rays of the sun.

One summer evening Tamanosuke was playing ball with the other pages in the palace garden. He was the best player of all, and people watched and admired his grace and skill. Suddenly his eyes grew haggard, his body began to tremble, and he was seized with convulsions in all his limbs. They took off his playing habit, and he seemed to have stopped breathing. When he regained consciousness, they bore him to his house. He grew worse and worse. His death seemed very near, and they despaired of saving him.

There was a certain samurai named Senzayemon Sasamura, a junior officer charged with the defence of the frontiers of the Province. No one took much notice of him. However, he loved Tamanosuke, though he had no means of sending him a message of love. He was waiting a favourable opportunity to declare his passion to him. When he learned of Tamanosuke's serious illness, he felt that he would not survive him if he should die.

Every morning he went to Tamanosuke's house and wrote his name on the register in the vestibule, like all the other samurai. He came again in the afternoon and in the evening after his supper to inquire after him. In this way he made three visits every day for six months.

Tamanosuke recovered. He washed himself in a bath and carefully shaved himself. After a meticulous toilet he went to the Lord to announce his recovery, and to thank him for the kindness he had shown to him while he was ill. Then he visited all those who had been good to him, and, after his round of visits, returned home. Finally, he told Kakubeï to bring him the register of visitors, and there he saw the name of Senzayemon Sasamura, and noticed that he had been three times a day from the beginning of his illness. He asked Kakubeï who this Senzayemon might be, and Kakubeï answered : ' He is not very well known. He must be an inferior samurai. He seemed to be really anxious about you. When I told him that my master was better, his face quite brightened ; but when I told him that the illness was getting worse, he grew pale and was overcome with distress. He was different from the ordinary visitors.'

Tamanosuke said : ' He is a very faithful individual, although I have never seen him.' And he went at once to Senzayemon's house, although it was far enough away, and said to the servant : ' I have come to thank Senzayemon for his kindness during my illness.'

95

Senzayemon ran joyfully to him and said : 'How good you are to have come so far to thank me for my insignificant actions. I am quite confused by your visit, Lord. But your health is not yet strong, and the evening air is fresh. I beg you to return to your house and take care of yourself.'

Tamanosuke answered : ' The world is so vain and uncertain, and man is like the momentary gleam of a light. In the morning we do not know surely if we shall live till the evening. I beg you to let me come in ; I have a private matter to discuss with you.'

Senzayemon led him to his room, and then Tamanosuke said to him : ' I am truly grateful for your devotion during my long illness. Forgive me for saying it frankly, but if you love me, humble as I am, I have come to be loved by you this evening, Senzayemon.'

Senzayemon blushed with pleasure : ' My heart cannot express itself in words. I pray you to go and see it. It is in the shrine of the god Hatjiman, who is the god of war and of soldiers. I consecrated it there, my lover.'

Tamanosuke went to the shrine, and asked the priest what was there. The priest said : ' Senzayemon gave me a box which contained his daily prayer for his friend's recovery.' Tamanosuke, with leave, opened the box and found

in it a dagger of Sadamune and a fervent prayer
for his recovery in a letter addressed to the god.
In this manner he discovered that he owed his
recovery to Senzayemon's prayer. Then he and
Senzayemon became faithful lovers.

Little by little this story spread, and came to the
ears of the Lord, who sentenced the two lovers
to be confined in their own houses. They were
both ready to die for their love, and did not at
all fear death. They calmly awaited their severe
punishment, and succeeded in finding a secret
means of corresponding with each other. A
year passed in this way.

Then, on the ninth of March, they sent a petition
to the Lord, in which they begged to be allowed
an honourable death by Hara-kiri. They
awaited their condemnation from moment to
moment. But one day a messenger came from
the Lord to Tamanosuke and ordered him to
become a samurai instead of the page that he
had been. Senzayemon was also pardoned.
They were very grateful to this Lord, and
decided to forgo their meetings until Tamano-
suke should have reached the age of twenty-
five. They no longer even spoke to
each other when they met in the
street. They but continued
to serve their Lord
faithfully.

The Author — All these tales are the work of Saïkaku Ihara, who lived in Japan during the seventeenth century, being born in 1642 and dying in 1693. They are mainly chosen from his *Glorious Tales of Pederasty*, though some are from *Tales of the Samurai Spirit* and *Tales of the Duty of a Samurai*, and one from *Stories in Letters*. I have translated them from the recently published and quite unique French version of Ken Sato. The significance of the tales is discussed in my terminal essay, where further information about their author will also be found.

3   *Shyôgun* — Regent, governor in general.

17   *facings* — The samurai wore a kind of reversed collar, shaped as two triangles, falling like wings on each shoulder. The clothes worn by Ukyo are those prescribed for Hara-kiri.

30   *great badger* — In old Japanese belief the badger had supernatural powers, and pursued men in some horrible shape.

98

*Songs of
the Geishas*

INTRODUCTORY NOTE

THE *following verses are definitely popular ones. They are folk-songs, almost music-hall songs, and are taken solely from the singing repertoire of Geishas. These girls have usually been sold into the trade by their parents, and their one desire is to be released by purchase or marriage. Release is the keynote of all their singing. It should be remembered, too, that practically all the Japanese poems with which we have been made familiar in English are classical and written to one or other of very strict rules, whereas these songs for the samisen are technically free. They have therefore no strict literary justification, and I trust that, even in second-hand translation, they may not seem to need one. I have selected some of my ninety from* Le Livre des Geishas *of Gaston Morphy, and the rest from* Chansons des Geishas *by Steinilber-Oberlin and Hidetake-Iwamura.*

Songs of the Geishas

1. Campanula.

Eglantine and campanula furtively
Placed in a letter, a moon setting
Beyond the plain, dew on the grass,
I wait.
Matsumushi singing of night, the late night,
Bell far sounds, and the crying of the wild geese,
All these things are love.

2. Cherry.

A horse tied by the bridle
To a flowering cherry.
When he shakes his head
There falls a snow of flowers,
Flower snow,
A snow of flowers.

3. Notes taken in my Bedroom.

Called out by the rushes
I go to my doorstep
And there is dew.

Troubled heart and coloured chrysanthemums,
Their deep scent is troubling
And their gold colour.

How pleasant is the scent of sake
With a chrysanthemum petal floating.
White frost is on the opened petal
And the frost has
  Coloured and deep
    Transparencies.

4. *Do Not Go.*

In the morning I hid his overcoat.
Your overcoat is playing hide and seek.
It is raining so. Look at the green rice field
Where the wet frogs are singing.

5. *Frog.*

I wish to keep him, but he will go to his own.
I call him back, but he goes to his own.
A frog jumps and goes to his own rice field
And the water there.
The world is leaving me. Night rain.

6. *Heart.*

My heart, a fine rain,
Life is so uncertain,
Drop by drop in the mist.

One is very handsome,
And the other may be more sincere.

This downfalling of leaves,
I shall never have any luck,
I will always be alone.
A stag cries and tramples the red leaves
Of the red maple. My heart is torn.

7. *Joy of Obscurity.*

Very little happiness would be enough ;
I see myself walking in a snow storm to her
With a net of new carps on my shoulder.
I would have paper garments
And, on windy Winter nights
When the plovers cry,
Also have my little flaming brazier of pine cones,
My little red portable brazier.
I could not do without that.
It is true, is it not,
That I could not do without that ?

8. *Prediction.*

A hole in the paper wall,
Who has been so guilty ?
Through it I hear the breaking of a samisen
string,
Meaning bad luck.

Yet the prediction-seller says
That mine is excellent.

9. *Unstable Love*

Love is unstable. I dream of a drifting
Barque. My body is limited.
My thought is infinite.
Things do not go as I would have them.
I see him in the dream of a light sleep
Or resting on one arm in place of a pillow.
Audible are the bells of Mii.

10. *Tamagava River.*

I bathed my snow skin
In pure Tamagava river.
Our quarrel is loosened slowly,
And he loosens my hair.
I am all uncombed.
I will not remember him,
   I will not altogether forget him,
      I will wait for Spring.

11. *Katushika.*

At Katushika the river water
Runs gently, and the plum blossom
Bursts out laughing.
The nightingale cannot withstand so many joys
And sings, and we are reconciled.
Our warm bodies touch,
   Cane branch and pine branch,
      Our boat floats in toward the bank.

12. *Blackness.*

The night is black
And I am excited about you.
My love climbs in me, and you ask
That I should climb to the higher room.
Things are hidden in a black night.
Even the dream is black
On the black-lacquered pillow,
Even our talk is hidden.

13. *Models.*

Butterfly
Or falling leaf,
Which ought I to imitate
In my dancing?

14. *Ghosts.*

Midnight uncalm shadows
Creaking the willow.
I am afraid.
This firefly
That has come to rest on my sleeve.
How strange it is,
How strange it all is.

15. *Snow Dance.*

The snow dances endlessly,
The snow falls in a whirlwind
Endlessly.
The wind-screen being put up
Provides our coming together.

Our bed of triple down
With its silk embroidered in butterflies and
peewees,
My young lover.

The perch-bird with the tender bill
Comes back to perch.

16. *Cats.*

With no care for duty or people
Or strange looks or the opinion of other cats,
One striped and the other white
Go on the edge of the roof
Or climb to the ridge of it.

Driven by the need of love
Which is stronger than death.

One day the wind of Autumn shall come
And they will not know each other.
My soul, I envy the love of cats.

17. *Night Waiting.*

I have waited all night.
It is midnight and I burn for love.
Towards dawn I pillow my head on my folded
arms
In case I may see him in dream.
I hate these blustering birds.

18. *Intimacy.*

Two in their little room
Far from other people and from life.
The silence of boiling water,
And she says : ' Listen to the wind
In the pine tops.'

19. *Small Hours.*

Midnight has passed and she wakes
And looks to left and right,
There is no one.
She only sees the long sleeve of her nightgown
To left and right.

20. *Knots in the Bamboo.*

The nightingale
Climbing a bamboo stem
Sings his love at every knot,
At every knot of it.

The season of long night is coming
When the leaves of the sainfoin redden.
I weep at every midnight.

21. *The Letter.*

If there were no moon
I would read it by the Winter snow light,
Or in Summer by the fireflies,
Or if there were no moon or snow or fireflies
I would read it by the light of my heart.

22. *Spring all in Flower.*

Spring all in flower
And the dark stain of the pine forest
On the watershed of the Sumida.
The gracious cherry trees reflected
In that deep water, which is love.
To-day two Chinese ducks
Float in the thread of the current,
And I too am married.

23. *Feast of Kamo.*

At the feast of Kamo
I put rose-mallows in my hair ;
He never came back, and I am waiting.
Time has a way of piling long days,
Long days, long days
Into a great hill.

24. *Return.*

I know she is light and faithless,
But she has come back half repentant
And very pale and very sad.
A butterfly needs somewhere to rest
At evening.

25. *A Single Cry.*

A flight of flying cuckoos
Across the moon, a single cry.
Is the moon crying cuckoo?
Night pales slowly. Men are cruel
And women are not.
They weep and say over sorrow
For a small separation.

26. *The Mat.*

She sulkily pretends to sleep,
Turning her back;
Suddenly the pretty slender music
Of a samisen delicately fingered.
Reconciliation. Where is her comb?
But there are dawn bells.
Separation, and always, always separation,
A boat puts out on a lake of the Yoshiwara.

27. *Dead Flower or Living.*

Last night a peach petal was wetted by the rain,
And when a girl
After her toilet said :
' Which is the more beautiful,
I or the peach petal ? '
And he said :
' Peach petal wetted by the rain is incomparable,'
There were tears and a tearing of flowers.

To taste the living flower
To-night would be quite a good night, my lord,
If so you wish.

28. *Alone.*

The device of the two copper plums
With silver in them
Slowly and very slowly
Satisfies.
Just as all finishes
Dew falls on my clenched hand.
I would rather the bean flowered yellow
And he were here.

29. *Shut In.*

Cherry flowers do not touch
The old stones of the wall.

From the Japanese

I am shut in here.
I am very much shut in here.
There is a part of the trap
Where the rat need not touch the curd.
The cherry trees are rose beyond Fuji.

30. *Since.*

What has happened to my thoughts
Since I knew you?
That is easy.
Until I met you I had no thoughts.

31. *After.*

After he left me,
Two pillows,
One body.
Where is he now?
He must be getting on for Komagata.
Damn that cuckoo.

32. *Night Rain.*

Sad night rain, I count the straws in the mat,
He will come, he won't come.
I twist a paper frog. Does it stand?
It falls down.
A vague presentiment.

The little lamp goes down and up,
Its oil exhausted.
He was always capricious.
Ah, my soul, that is his voice.

33. *Madam Moon.*

The moon is digustingly modest
Under a great cloud
When I am waiting,
And when he comes
She spitefully breaks forth.
You are jealous, Madam Moon,
But we have had a few black nights
When you were lazy.

34. *Weariness.*

The pale day
Pierces the bamboo blind.
Grief pierces my heart
And I count the bands of light
Not knowing why,
Like that.

35. *Annoyed.*

Really I am annoyed this time
And I have left her.
But the weeping willow wept at my door
And quenched my anger.

From the Japanese

When the Spring rain has ceased
I will go back to her in moonlight,
But discreet moonlight and much veiled
I pray.

36. Crickets.

Autumn casts herself carelessly over the earth
In a brocade of many colours,
And yet it is just now
That the crickets begin to change their cry to :
' Patch those rags, patch those rags.'
I think they carry economy
Almost too far.

37. Emotion.

There is white frost on the pond
And on the grass.
There is light mist.
I walk on frozen leaves that go crack
And my heart beats
And it is delightful.

38. Moonlight.

I detest my phantom shadow
In the bright moon.
I look, thinned out by love,
And think, smoothing my hair :
Am I really as thin as that ?

39. *Quick Hours.*

Wet in the rain of morning.
You are still in my arms.
The hours in bed are quick hours.
See, how delightful I look with this paper on
my brow
As a bride's headdress.
What pet name
Will you give me when we are married?
But you have gone to sleep again
And do not hear the evening bell.

40. *Green Willow.*

The breeze is so light
That when it soothes the green willow
It seems not to touch her.
Indistinct shadow.
We have set our two pillows
Very close in the bed.

Our mornings and our evenings.

And our useless little quarrels
And then our letters.
Is waiting or parting bitterer?

Let us not separate.

41. *His Pretty Gesture.*

Because of his pretty gesture
I have fallen completely in love with him.

My letter written in common character
Will be worth more than a verbal message.
But I may not hold him yet.
I am going to drink sake all night
Without bothering to warm it.

I lie down on the floor
Just where I am, and sleep.
I wake with a start
To hear the night watch crying :
' Fire, take care of fire ! '

42. *Bamboo.*

The sparrow is excellently
At home with the bamboo.
One day the bamboo is shaped into a snare
And catches the sparrow.
Is that not so ?

43. *Two Fan Game.*

Two thrown fans
Have fallen across each other.
It is a good sign.

I see two mortals close in each other's arms
Like two leaves fallen together.

Will he be a fine chrysanthemum?
I will put him in a vase
And look at him.
He will be plum blossom
Having both scent and colour.

44. *Since this Morning.*

At little day
I am cold.
A maple leaf
Planes down and settles silently.

The things one believes.

I have hated day
Since this morning:
His insensitive glance
Looked at me coldly
Like the pale dawn moon.

45. *Who Loves.*

A body that loves
Is fragile and uncertain,
A floating boat.
The fires in the fishing boats at night
Burn red, my heart burns red.

Wooden stakes hold up the nets
Against the tide of Uji.

The tide is against me.

46. *Nightingale Sings to Plum Tree.*

How the nightingales sing to the plum trees
And the frogs splash in the water.
That is love.
The call of people and of things
Is everywhere.

Dark clouds,
Fishing boats,
At the will of the tide,
At the will of the wind.

They seem to move their own sails.
The ropes are woven in the old way
Like woman's hair.

Deep down in green reflections.

Ah, back her to the port of love !

47. *Life.*

To the passing dawn ?
To a boat passing ?
To the wake the boat leaves ?
To the froth the wake leaves ?

48. *Hiding Place.*

No more grieving.
I hide myself in my happiness
As a firefly
Hides in a moon ray.

49. *Rupture.*

Steps die on the brittle leaves,
I think of very much.
Evening, a perched crow
On a bare branch.
The end of Autumn.

50. *Plum Tree Under Snow.*

The plum tree still lives,
Even still blossoms
Under the snow ; my heart,
My most unfortunate heart
Also.

51. *Rose Chrysanthemum.*

Three butterflies
On a rose chrysanthemum.
The white flies away,
The red flies away,
The black lights on my garment.
Meaning ?

52. *Firefly.*

This evening I caught a firefly
To light my waiting soul
And for amusement.
My right hand covers the firefly in my left
And both are transparent and rosy
Because of it.
How funny !

53. *In the Spring Rain.*

The nightingale is quite wet
In the Spring rain.
The scent of the flowers of the plum tree
Rises at every beating
Of the wet wing.

Nightingales that play with flowers,
How charming that is.

Some birds do not know
Where they may nest at evening,
But I am a nightingale
And my master is a plum tree.

Soon I shall be free of my body,
Free to love. Is not that so ?
And nothing else matters.

54. *O Dreams.*

O dreams, do not bring me
The face of my girl in sleep.
My waking and my pain
Would quite unman me.

55. *Flakes of Flowers.*

It is snowing, Winter,
It is snowing.
But the flakes
Are flowers also.
See, it is already Spring
By the cloud way.

56. *Surugi Lake.*

Dew from the lotuses
Of Surugi Lake
Goes up in a light fume.
My hope becomes lighter than air
And disappears.
Yet a voice is saying : ' Who knows ?
Soon he may marry you.'

57. *Maple Leaves.*

Do you know why the Autumn moon
Spreads her desirable brightness
On the hill ?

It is so that we two may count the leaves of the
maple
Falling
One by one.

58. *Deep Light.*

I have no wish for
A frivolous or coquettish existence,
I want the deep life of love.

I have set up the double screen
Against a wind balmed with the plum trees.

Come to me and I will love you
In the tender light of a veiled moon,
I will love you, far from the plum trees.

Yet afterwards in bed
I know I shall sulk and weep ;
Frogs in the garden pool
All night, all night.

59. *Snow Night.*

There are two in the small room
On this cold snow night.
Pretty half-meanings
As they tease each other,
Hair she has just washed
And cannot manage.
' You get on my nerves,' she says,
' Always chewing your toothpick.'

60. *Spring Night.*

This dream of a Spring night
Grows complicated.
The smell of his body lies on the air.
The cloudy sky and my ringed eyes
Are veiled.
Are we not a couple
Made of flower and butterfly ?
Well, well, I mean to say.

61. *Love Night.*

The cuckoo has sung all night
And at first they did not sleep at all.
There is sweet slumber after love
With a rounded arm for pillow.
The lamp was fetched away
Without their noticing.

62. *Moon and Plum Tree.*

The moon and the plum tree part not
On a very clear night,
But rather lie smiling to the snow.
Not a word is said,
But the scent the plum tree cannot hold
Goes up toward the moon.
And look at the innocent whiteness
Of the plum tree.

63. *Bamboos and Sparrows.*

This sparrow lighting
Harmoniously
On the bamboo.
In love things do not go quite so
Harmoniously.
It is I alone who love and suffer.
I hate his beastly face.

64. *Sky before Dawn.*

Sky just at dawn between the trees
The cuckoo flies and hides.
I comb the wet hair on my temples
I am wetted and am happy.
I am so wet.
It rains this morning.

65. *Myosotis.*

If I clasp my hands, my sleeve :
Dew and perfume and colour.
His picture remains in absence
Myosotis, memory.
If he flowered on a branch
I would plant him,
And love him every
Lonely hour.

66. *Flower of the Cherry.*

It is because they fall
That they are admirable.
What is the good of clinging
Without hope?
Clinging violently to the branches,
Withered on all the branches,
Soiled by the birds.

67. *Pillow.*

How many nights
We have not come together.
The plovers of Awaji island
Mingle their crying.
I am alone and wretched
In this plank custom's hut,
Alone and lost.
That moonbeam entering to my pillow,
Would it were,
Just for once.

68. *The Pine Tree.*

The wind in the roof
Is playing on three strings,
Moon, snow and flower.

From the Japanese

Right from the very small
Pushing of the Spring
The green of the green pine
Changes not.
What do the infant cranes cry
Fluttering from the nest
In the green pine top ?
' Long live the King ! ' they cry.
The green pine lives for ever.

69. *Kawai, Kawai.*
(*My dear, my dear*)

The firefly singing not
Burns in silence ;
She suffers more
Than the loud insect who says :
' Kawai, kawai ! '
Why have I given all my soul
To a man without sincerity ?
I regret it, I rather regret it.

70. *Notes taken in my Bedroom.*

It must be late
Autumn night
The moon falls
Wind is cold.

My dwarf harp, my little koto
Is by me on the pillow,
Lying lightly.
I flutter a chord
On the seven strings.

I hear the first wild goose crying :
' We have come back, come back.'
It is very late.

71. *Wanting to Write a Letter.*

I want to send him a letter
But do not know what to write.
Tell me something,
White paper.

72. *Heat.*

Noon on feet of felt
Has come into the city.
Not a leaf stirs.
On the rope of the temple bell
A butterfly is sleeping.

73. *Bindweed.*

Every morning
You flower with new colours
And garland the well bucket,
Your petals are eyes
Blinded with dew.

130

From the Japanese

You are delightful.

Flower long, flower differently,
Emerald cup.

74. *Faith.*

I am the ordinary cherry tree
Whose flower is single.
It blossoms in the plain.
I am not one of those double
Cherry trees.

75. *If you Promise.*

If you promise, do it lightly.
Look at the maple leaves.
The light resist,
The heavy break away
And fall.
Is that not so ?

76. *South-East Quarter.*

Light affairs become frivolous
At Fukagawa,
My body is frivolous.

A thin, uncoloured chord on the samisen.

In intimate Nakatcho Street
Affairs are private,
And the news of our love
Spreads gallantly,
The way of the South-East.

Two lovers are in the little room
And the screen has double hinges.

We pretend worldly fidelity,
Painting moles on each other.

Perhaps
We shall know in heaven.

77. *Dew and Rush.*

The dew pretends she
Loves the love of the rush,
The rush that he loves no dew.
But the rush will blossom
And both understand.

78. *Wonder.*

If I think she loves me
The snow is light
On my umbrella.
Crying plovers,
Dishevelled wind.

79. *Joy.*

Visitor this evening
We run up the long corridor
Clicking of clogs.

Only one man,
Only one person to be loved.

I go back to my room,
Retreat, honour,
Lacquered pillow,
Silence.

I hear the watchman's rattle,
Laughter in the next room.

80. *Under Snow.*

Flowers under the snow
Scarcely betray their colour.
We meet and she smiles and is silent.
' If I must die,' she is thinking,
' I will die of love
As the snow dies.'

81. *Before my Birds.*

I moan for love
Before my birds.
They also are in a cage.

My small complaints
Are sorry like mouse cries.
The birds hop forward to tease me
And I like it,
Being so shut in.

The sake is cold
Because my torment
Makes me inefficient.
There is such a thing as great grief,
Such a thing as
Being shut in.

82. *Getting out of Bed.*

He rises and goes.   There are
Rather dark clouds.
Shall I be noisy cricket
Or firefly burning in silence,
Dumb grief or tearful parting?

And when I think we might
Never have met,
Been utter strangers.

83. *Spring Branches.*

Spring flowers at the branch end
Over the water.
Love is very deep,
Their reflection is very deep.

From the Japanese

I had to wet my sleeves
To gather them,
And I want to go on
Wetting, wetting, wetting my sleeves.

84. *First Snow.*

This first snow
Is very white
Like first love.
My maid asks from the doorstep :
' Where shall I throw
The tea-leaves ? '

85. *Bed.*

Under the unnecessarily large
Mosquito curtain
My little heart
Is fiercer than a nightlight.

86. *Then.*

The flowers come to blossom, then
We look at the flowers, then
They wither, then——

Other TUT BOOKS available:

SUN-DIALS AND ROSES OF YESTERDAY *by Alice Morse Earle*

THE TEN FOOT SQUARE HUT AND TALES OF THE HEIKE: Being Two Thirteenth-century Japanese classics, the "Hojoki" and selections from the "Heike Monogatari" *translated by A. L. Sadler*

THE TOURIST AND THE REAL JAPAN *by Boye de Mente*

TYPHOON! TYPHOON! An Illustrated Haiku Sequence *by Lucile M. Bogue*

UNBEATEN TRACKS IN JAPAN: An Account of Travels in the Interior Including Visits to the Aborigines of Yezo and the Shrine of Nikko *by Isabella L. Bird*

Please order from your bookstore or write directly to:

CHARLES E. TUTTLE CO., INC.
Suido 1-chome, 2–6, Bunkyo-ku, Tokyo 112

or:

CHARLES E. TUTTLE CO., INC.
Rutland, Vermont 05701 U.S.A.